The SCIENTIFIC Sufi

The SCIENTIFIC Sufi

THE LIFE & TIMES OF
Jagadish Chandra Bose

MEHER WAN

PENGUIN
VIKING
An imprint of Penguin Random House

VIKING

USA | Canada | UK | Ireland | Australia
New Zealand | India | South Africa | China | Singapore

Viking is part of the Penguin Random House group of companies whose addresses can be found at global.penguinrandomhouse.com

Published by Penguin Random House India Pvt. Ltd
4th Floor, Capital Tower 1, MG Road,
Gurugram 122 002, Haryana, India

First published in Viking by Penguin Random House India 2023

10 9 8 7 6 5 4 3 2

ISBN 9780670098057

Typeset in Adobe Garamond Pro by Manipal Technologies Limited, Manipal
Printed at Replika Press Pvt. Ltd, India

www.penguin.co.in

To the great fathers

From the Temple of Science in the West,
far across the Indus,
oh, my friend, you have brought
the garland of victory,
decorated the humbled head
of the poor mother . . .

Today, the mother has sent blessings
in words of tears,
of this unknown poet.
Amidst the great Scholars
of the West, brother,
these words will reach only your ears.

—Rabindranath Tagore

---

* From 'Kalpana' in *Rabindra Rachanabali* (Bengali), Vol. 7. Calcutta: Visva-Bharati, 1975, p. 157.

Contents

Preface

Jagadish Chandra Bose is considered to be the 'Father of Modern Science in India'. He had chosen to do his research work in India and had refused several lucrative offers from the West to shift his lab work despite the humiliation and extreme resistance he faced for his research in India. He had achieved and established the tall standards not only for India but also for researchers worldwide. The greatest leaders of the then scientific world praised him and his research tirelessly while he was simultaneously demeaned in his own country. A nationalist to the core, he set the stage for modern science and technology in India and also made the countrypersons proud by earning the respect of the greatest from around the world. Several of his students got nominated for the Nobel Prize for their scientific contributions while working in India. Sir J.C. Bose worked till his last breath and sacrificed everything for his country and people. He did not participate in the big political movements, nor did he acquire fame among revolutionaries, but his style of resistance was unique and one of a kind.

The effort to bring out his biography is an attempt to present the life and ideas of Sir J.C. Bose before people so that they can get inspiration from his life. I do not claim that it is a complete biography of Sir Jagadish Chandra Bose. The life of such a great man cannot be compiled in a few hundred pages. It is just an effort to highlight the spirit of one of the greatest people of Indian history, whom we have almost forgotten. I have wept, been thrilled, felt proud and got goosebumps numerous times when I was researching and writing this book. I have tried my best to put aside my own experiences, prejudices and opinions. My attempt has been to present his persona through the events in his life, his thoughts, his times and his contemporaries.

—Dr Meher Wan

1

The Buried Sparks

It was the latter half of the nineteenth century. The business and administration of the British were flourishing in the Indian subcontinent. The British were planning to start the railways in their residencies. Efforts to establish industries compatible with Indian resources and diaspora had already been going on. To run these industries, skilled labour was needed. The British Raj was established in most of India. On the lower administration level . Indian natives were running the British government. Several kings and supremos of princely states were now functioning merely as tax collectors of the British. The large *riyasats* were divided into districts and *parganas* and faithful Indians were appointed there as high authority officers. People and the kings of India both had accepted the British rule. Everything seemed to be going fine, but 90-year-old Lalon Faqir understood the innuendo of a silent fire burning inside the people. When he used to roam around in the villages of Bengal and sing on his Tanpura, wise people would understand that Lalon Faqir was not only talking about spiritual slavery.

মন তুই রইলি খাঁচার আসে
খাঁচা যে তোর কাঁচা বাঁশের
কোন দিন খাঁচা পড়বে খসে
ফকির লালন কেঁদে কয়।

Oh, my soul! thou living with the highest expectations,
But your cage is fragile,
One fine day, this cage will also be shattered
Lalon says,
The bird has already flown out through the skylight above the door.

Buried sparks inside took the form of cinder. In 1857, the native sepoy of Meerut and Barrackpore revolted against the British. This revolt quickly spread in several crucial cantonments of the British. On 16 May 1857, the sepoy and workers of the palace murdered fifty-two Europeans in cold blood inside the Delhi castle. The sepoy opened the prison doors and set hundreds of prisoners free. Clouds of chaos covered North India. The spark against British slavery, which was just inside a few people, started creating a smog in the skies of northern British India. People started uniting themselves against the British. With this spirit, the people of different riyasats and areas of the subcontinent, divided within and fighting each other for no significant reasons, realized that they must unite against the British for their common good. A public movement against the British started shaping itself with increased political consciousness. India also started taking shape as a country, culturally and politically. The East India Company couldn't handle this hostile situation, and it had to hand over the rule to the British Empire to control the state of affairs. The spark of mutiny, which twinkled in Barrackpore, was now burning in Kanpur, Jhansi, Meerut and Delhi and was spreading towards Ambala. The rebels announced Bahadur Shah Zafar as the king of India but it did not last long and the British brutally crushed the mutiny. Countless people were killed and several kings were either slaughtered or became captives as prisoners of war. This oppression fuelled unrest among the common public.

The time was not so good for native Indian officers in the British government—the sepoy used to refuse to parade—the attacks on the families of the British had increased. The common public, which had been happily obeying the British, had accepted them as their rulers and helped them rule over themselves, was not behaving, so now and became a deadly puzzle for the British. Nobody could guess which Indian sepoy or officer or house help who work in British houses would kill how many white people or set fire to their colonies. The rebelling public of the country started detesting and downgrading the Indians loyal to the British and it became complex for brown officers to help the British in ruling India. It was one of the most challenging times for the brown officers as fellow Indians started detesting them and the British were doubting their loyalty.

When the fire of rebellion was raging in West Bengal, many areas of North Bengal were still tranquil. An order from the governor of the Bengal Residency arrived at the Faridpur district office, not far from Dhaka, the then capital of North Bengal. In the order, the officers were instructed to be alert and prepare to identify and deal with the mass rebellion before it flared up. This order was received by Bhagban Chandra Bose, the deputy magistrate of Faridpur. He was famous as a brilliant, strong, loyal and kind officer. Tales of his administrative intelligence and bravery were told in the region. In the nineteenth century, a district magistrate had to look after all the district's affairs. In these services, such people were selected by the British who apart from delivering justice, had an intellectual and deep understanding of the local area and the ability to smoothly to run the British rule in India. Such a candidate was needed for this post, who could also fight the dacoits, rebels, etc. with the help of the police force and his people, if required. Bhagban Chandra Bose lived up to all these parameters. He had received modern western education, and the rural man in him was still alive. He was trusted by the British, and he also had deep love and care for the people of his district. He was respected among the public because of his new schemes and their implementation for the people's good. Known for his honesty, Bhagban Chandra Bose used to help people on many occasions by giving them money from his own salary. It is said that people used to go to his office without hesitation with their problems and no one returned dissatisfied.

The ancestral home of Bhagban Chandra Bose was in the village of Rarikhal in the Bikrampur area of Munshiganj Parganas, which was about 100 km from his office, and around 16 km away from Dhaka. This area had been remarkably fertile due to its location in the Terai region of the Padma River. The local public was financially prosperous. Since Bhagban Chandra Bose grew up in this area, he understood the demography well. The Muslim population was high here, but the Hindus were also prosperous. People of both religions lived in harmony.

A vast *Buddha-Vihara* had been found in the excavations in the area around Bikrampur. The period of this Buddha-Vihara is believed to be about a thousand years ago from today. There was also a Buddhist influence on the local culture. It is said that about a thousand years ago, there came a time when fanaticism was increasing among the people of both Hindu and Muslim religions, and they were going on killing each other. At this time, many people here adopted the Sufi sect, and believed that caste or religion was not necessary for the attainment of God. Singing these thoughts through Sufi songs and music, the saints wandered from one place to another. Bengal's 'Baul' music flourished during this time, whose roots are believed to be associated with Buddhism. Due to these reasons, this area was culturally very vibrant. The famous Sufi saint Lalon Faqir (1772–1890) established an ashram in Kushtia, which was near Bikrampur. Lalon Faqir had become famous by then, and people started calling him Mahatma/Saint. Today, his place in Bengal is equal to that of Kabir. Bikrampur has been the *Vidyapeeth* (Seat of Learning) of North Bengal for a long time. There were schools for Sanskrit and Pali called *Tols* which exist even today. These can be considered contemporaries of the universities of ancient times. Students used to come here from far and wide to get the traditional education. Apart from this, there was also an astronomical observatory called '*Man Mandir*'. However, it is a wonder as to what was the reason to build an observatory here! Due to the abundance of rivers and canals, transport was mainly by water, and it was cheap. Economically and culturally, even the ordinary people of this region lived a happy life.

After the Sepoy Mutiny of 1857, dissatisfaction among the public was rapidly turning into a rebellion. It had been almost a year since the uprising began. A message was sent from the governor of the Calcutta Residency of the British government to all the ruled districts, asking them to keep an eye on possible insurgent attempts in their respective districts so that they could be controlled in time. Although there was peace in his district, and Mr Bose kept the people of his district as happy as possible, the place was not far from Calcutta, so the possibility of rebellion could not be ruled out. Bhagban Chandra Bose was worried due to the suppression of the rebels by the British. Apart from the main opponents, innocent people were also severely repressed. The British were very ruthless about this revolt, and they vehemently scoffed at the possibilities of revolution in other places. Conversely, there were reports of insurgents burning officers' houses from all over. The rebels were selectively attacking the family members of the officers.

Bhagban Chandra Bose was now on a double-edged sword. He had to spend more time in the office and district area. Mr Bose used to go from village to village and meet people, trying to know their state of mind. At the same time, he was worried about his family. His wife was pregnant, and in such a condition, she needed more care. Because of the attacks on the officers' houses and his busy-ness, he kept his wife in his native village Rarikhal, which was across the Padma River near Faridpur.

The British were able to suppress the revolt of 1857 immediately. By 1858, rebellions of Jhansi, Lucknow, Kanpur, Ambala, Ferozepur, Indore, Agra, Arrah and Kathiabar to Chittagong were trampled. Bahadur Shah Zafar, the emperor of Delhi and the leader of Delhi's rebels, was deported. On 7 October 1858, under the direction of Lieutenant Omani, Bahadur Shah Zafar, with a few of his family members, was taken on bullock carts to Calcutta and then to Rangoon in Burma by water route. When Bahadur Shah Zafar's convoy passed through Calcutta, there was an apprehension that the rebels might plan an attack. There was a high alert in Bengal, and all the officers were vigilant. When Bahadur Shah Zafar's convoy left for Rangoon from Calcutta, Bhagban Chandra Bose, Deputy Magistrate of Faridpur, also breathed a sigh of relief.

It was late at night, winter had knocked over East Bengal, and the sun was now returning from the sky a little sooner. When he was busy with his office work the next day, news came from the village that his wife had delivered a son. The person who gave the information said that the son was handsome and chubby and everyone was happy at home. The child's grandparents were distributing sweets among the village folks, giving gifts to the poor—they had gotten the heir of their family. He was the only male child of the Bose couple. The newborn's mother was waiting for her husband to come home. It was 30 November 1858. The pundits-astrologers of the village were rushing to Bose's home trying to predict the newborn's future. His father, Bhagban Chandra Bose, was also in a hurry to reach home.

2

Facing the fear

Nature's laws are extraordinary. It has its plan for everyone. Babies have to have a robust cry for some time after birth. We learn to laugh with time, but crying is our first action after birth. It is in our intrinsic nature. Immediately after delivery, the rapid crying of the baby clears the windpipe and activates the lungs so that the baby starts breathing properly. Every mother eagerly waits for her baby's first cries. Bamsundari Devi was also waiting for the same. It is said that this child remained silent for an unusually long time, then opened his eyes and looked around with a single glance—just as someone reaches another world in a flash and opens his eyes in a moment, surprised to see everything anew. The child was lying motionless, stunned in the light of the new world and the air in his lungs was getting impatient to come out. The midwife, the grandmother and the mother started worrying whether the child was born dead. Suddenly, the room reverberated with screams. Crying is a sign of life—it is possible to take birth on this earth without crying, but it is impossible to get a life without it. Bose's courtyard was filled with joy at the child's shrill cry.

Sitting next to the grandmother, Bhagban Chandra Bose listened to the story of the birth of his child. A small smile floated on his lips and his face appeared to glow. The person who used to work for and worry about the future of the children of his entire district now felt good thinking about his own child. Every father feels a little happy upon placing his unfulfilled dreams on his child's shoulders. When the child becomes successful in those dreams, the father feels the joy of winning himself. Bhagban Chandra Bose also had all the sweet and bitter experiences of life and all the dreams arising out of them, but he felt comforted just at the thought of handing them over to the newborn.

The boy was named Jagadish.

After birth, a newborn's body develops to keep pace with the earth's resources. There are traditions in the Hindu religion to celebrate certain physical and mental developmental stages. These traditions are called sacraments and they keep changing according to caste, religion and localities. When a baby develops its milk teeth, some light food—easily chewable and digestible—is given to the child apart from the mother's milk. The *Annaprasan* rite is significant for the children of Bengal. All the relatives gather at home for this ritual and worship together. After chanting mantras, the child is fed with anything other than milk for the first time. This ceremony takes place eight months after birth. Jagadish's grandmother used to massage the child by laying him in the sun—she would say that if her grandson was to become a deputy collector like his father, he would also have to fight with dacoits and would need a strong body for that. Eventually, the child started uttering sounds. He crawled on his chest, then on his knees and then tried to stand on his feet. In those days, there were no toys like baby-walkers. These toys and devices have taken away the feeling of learning to walk by falling. In childhood, two hands were always there to take care of little Jagadish. Slowly, the child started making a stir in the whole courtyard. His grandfather would take him for a walk in the fields early in the morning. He would keenly observe the new outside world. There were tiny flowers in the fields and butterflies hovering over them. There were many plants with different leaves, some big, some very small. Many trees on the side of the fields were many times bigger than a child. He was thrilled to see the shadow of the rising sun waver in the waves of the canal water.

Once, when young Jagadish was going towards the fields sitting on his grandfather's shoulders, his grandfather showed him a strange plant. As soon as he touched the plant, its leaves withered. Then the child touched the other leaves, and they too withered and shrank. Seeing this, the child was surprised and started laughing. He liked this plant. Suddenly, the child started worrying about the plant, and thought, 'Did this plant die? Will its leaves be like before? What happens to the leaves of this plant if we touch it?'

Jagadish grew with each passing day and the love and affection of his grandparents watered his growth. Jagadish loved the village and his childhood was adorned with its dirt and dust. Jagadish used to be amazed by worldly things and his explorations with his grandfather instilled new buds of knowledge in him. His grandfather used to listen to him attentively, answering all his curious questions.

Bhagban Chandra Bose wanted the child to stay with him now, so that he could be sent to school. Therefore, after making all the necessary arrangements in the village, he brought his wife and son to Faridpur. Jagadish would have been about three years old now. The house in Faridpur was much bigger and grander than the house in the village. There was the Padma River flowing behind the nearby garden. There were many trees and plants here and animals too. They had more modern facilities here than in the village. His mother was pleased to come with his father, but Jagadish's mind was dry. His father got busy with office work, his mother with household chores. There was no one to listen to Jagadish. He was also forbidden to go far out of the house. One always had to wear good clothes and behave decently, which Jagadish was not used to yet. He still liked to play with wet clay but he was no longer in the village.

In Faridpur, Jagadish observed the respect given to his father for the first time. When his father used to come to the village, his grandparents would often scold him for any little reason, but here, there was no one to scold his father. Everyone seemed to respect him, obey him and bow before him. After coming to Faridpur, Jagadish looked at Bhagban Chandra Bose with a new perception and realized that his father was a big man. One day, when Jagadish could not live with his thoughts, he went to his mother and asked her why everyone here obeyed father's words? His mother answered, '*Dadaji* is the head of his family in the village and everyone listens to him. Similarly, your father is the head of a vast family here—the people who respect him are all members of an extended family.' Jagadish was happy to know that but he had never seen such a big family. One consequence of this was that he would insist on meeting the whole family whenever it came to his mind, especially when he remembered his grandparents. He would become impatient to meet the grandparents of this big family.

Although most of the people of Faridpur lived a peaceful and prosperous life, dacoits and robbers dominated the place too at that time. Goods being transported for trade through the rivers were often looted. There was always a fear of dacoits and robbers among the traders. Being a deputy magistrate, this was always trouble for Bhagban Chandra Bose. His task was not only to settle judicial matters and to safeguard law and order, but also to fight dacoits with the help of troops. At that time, the responsibility of a collector was not just to look after the district for its smooth operation; the jurisdiction and responsibilities of a collector were much broader than today.

It had not been many days since Jagadish had come to Faridpur. In those days, the incidents of dacoities and robberies had increased in the jurisdiction of Bhagban Chandra Bose. Once, Mr Bose followed a lead and arrested a well-known dacoit with the help of a troop of soldiers handpicked by him. The dacoit's associates did not get a chance to cope with the sudden attack and a stampede broke out among them. In this stampede, the soldiers either killed or caught many dacoits. In this way, Bhagban Chandra Bose forced the leader of the dacoits to surrender and arrested him with his own hands.

When his father returned home late, the soldiers were accompanying him. Jagadish got scared seeing this. Later, when his mother explained everything to him, he felt proud of his father. She told him that there was no need to be afraid of the soldiers because they were also members of his father's extended family. Children usually perceive their fathers as heroes but it was not the same with Jagadish. His respect and affection for his father increased when he started to observe him closely. His father was not a frequent presence in Faridpur, which is why Jagadish could not get along with him very well. How can he find time for his family when he is so preoccupied with his responsibilities? But in Jagadish's mind, a kind of hypnotic affection for his father was starting to arise. He would now go to his father and try to talk to him. He would try to engage him in his child-friendly quirks, making strange requests to his father. His father also tried to listen to Jagadish properly but the closeness between father and son was not that great. It took some time for him to get close to his father. Relationships only cook well on a low flame.

Being situated on the banks of the river, life at Faridpur was heavily dependent on water. People would catch fish and the river water would help produce paddy. The diet of local people was mainly based on fish and rice. Local transport was primarily based on the river. There were long, thick forests along the riverbanks and boats would go from one place to another through the river surrounded by dense forests. This part of the river was stunning. Bhagban Chandra Bose also had a garden on the banks of the river in which there were different types of plants. Bhagban Chandra Bose was fond of gardening. He used to tell Jagadish about different kinds of plants. Jagadish had found an old friend here too—the tickling plant. Here, there was big bush of *Lajjavati* which he had seen with his grandfather in Rarikhal.

During the holidays, the whole family used to eat food while sitting on the ghats of the river. One day, his father took Jagadish to the market, where Jagadish saw all kinds of fish. The child had no idea that the outside world was so big. Gradually, Jagadish's hesitation with his father went on decreasing. Whenever his father would leave the house, Jagadish would insist on going out with him. Now, he didn't hesitate to ask his father awkward questions. He kept collecting questions throughout the day. Bhagban Chandra Bose, who arrived late at night, exhausted, attempted to respond to the child with his knowledge and experience.

Time passed and Jagadish now had a sister. Jagadish showered all his love on his newborn sister. It was like he had found a new toy. Jagadish would have many questions regarding the newborn sister (later Mrs M.M. Bose). When I was a little kid, could I also not even speak? Could I cry? Did I only drink mother's milk? Why doesn't she eat rice? Why can't a newborn eat rice? Why doesn't she have teeth? Why do teeth come out on their own after a few months? Who pushes them out? Why is that my blood is red and locusts' blood white? Why do we have blood? Do plants have blood? Time was passing fast. Jagadish became engrossed in Faridpur.

Once, it was late at night and everyone in the house had slept. Suddenly, the guards of the bungalow started shouting out to the Deputy Magistrate Sahib. It was too late by the time his wife woke Bhagban Chandra Bose from his deep sleep. The house was on fire and it was quickly spreading throughout the bungalow. In a hurry, everything in the house was taken out. Bose started searching for necessary papers and his wife searched for ornaments, money, etc. The children, still asleep, were taken outside the house in haste. The servants of the house were helping. The fire spread very fast and Bhagban Chandra Bose was clueless. All that was found in a jiffy was taken out. Everyone had come out. Neighbours also came to the rescue, most of whom were Muslims. In this chaos, a man said to Bhagban Chandra Bose, 'You would not like us to touch your idol, but I think it can be saved.' Actually, it was not any idol, it was Jagadish's younger sister—she had been left on the bed in the chaos. Seeing so much fire, she was astonished and frozen, her face became expressionless. She didn't even cry. She was rescued quickly. Luckily, she was not harmed by the fire. Nobody expected the fire, so they were not prepared. Everything had burnt down in that fire, from everyday items to jewellery, clothes, etc. The cowshed and the stable behind the house burnt down and turned to ash along with the animals in it. The Bose family faced this disaster with incredible difficulty. They had to live in the tiny old house of a Muslim neighbour until their bungalow was rebuilt. Some gave them clothes, some gave utensils for cooking. Everyone was helping Bhagban Chandra Bose.

The house was deliberately set on fire by someone. It was set alight by sprinkling inflammable material from all sides of the bungalow. Thus, the fire spread very fast. After investigating, Bhagban Chandra Bose came to know about the one who set the fire. Many years ago, he had heard the case of a notorious dacoit and had sentenced him to rigorous imprisonment. The dacoit became quite furious after hearing the sentence. He had threatened Deputy Magistrate Bhagban Chandra Bose while leaving the court. He and his companions would take revenge on the judge as soon as he came out of jail. It was he who had set this terrible fire.

Incidents of dacoity were a part of everyday life in Faridpur and tales of terrors by dacoits were a part of daily conversation. Dacoits were dangerous around Dhaka and Faridpur. It was challenging to deal with them. The crop yield was higher due to irrigation and fertile soil in this area, thus, more incidents of loot. The dense forests and rivers provided a favourable environment for hiding and long-term camping. The dacoits found it easiest to rob merchants and ordinary people. They would kidnap someone and then ask for a high amount of ransom. The gangs of dacoits were so powerful that they did not find it very difficult to hide the dead bodies of their victims in the area. One time, there was a lot of chaos in the district. Later, with the government's efforts, strict steps were taken against the dacoits. The force of the district was strengthened. Several people who had been involved in the dacoits' gangs in their youth were also recruited as state soldiers. They were now older but they had important information about dacoits and their activities. They had dacoity experiences which helped in fighting dacoits for the police.

Jagadish's childhood was also spent listening to the tales of the robberies. Since his father was in such a position that he had to face dacoits almost daily, there used to be tales of dacoits in the house too which indirectly affected Jagadish. He was afraid of dacoits initially. Hearing the dreaded stories of dacoits in his childhood and after the fire incident in the house, he was frightened to the core. Whenever there was a mention of dacoits, he would tremble with fear. In such a situation, his father would give him courage. He would tell stories of his fights with the dacoits, through which Jagadish would get some relief. Bhagban Chandra Bose was a superhero for his son. Like every 5–6 year old child, Jagadish had great faith in his father.

Once, there was an annual fair in Faridpur. Jagadish must have been 5 or 6 years old at that time. It was a celebration in every aspect. In the evening, there was *Ram-Leela*. During those days, there were discourses on *Ram-Katha* and wrestling competitions. People from different groups used to organize wrestling competitions. At that fair, a wrestling competition was held for the police personnel in which only policemen could participate but anyone could come to watch the wrestling. All its participants used to be tall and handsome policemen from North-East India. This type of wrestling was very famous in the surrounding areas, and the wrestlers used to practise for a long time for this. Bhagban Chandra Bose, the deputy magistrate of Faridpur, was invited to watch the final wrestling match. Bhagban Chandra Bose also took the boy, Jagadish, with him to watch the final match of wrestling.

The game started normally. Both the players were strong and well-versed in their sport. As time passed, it became hard to guess who was going to win. Both the players were making their bets—sometimes one would beat the other, and sometimes the other would beat the first. The boy, Jagadish, started enjoying wrestling. He was engrossed in the game and was encouraging the players by shouting. It seemed that this wrestling game would not end soon. But in no time, a wrestler made such a move that the second wrestler fell on his back and then he struck the fallen wrestler. People were taken aback. They didn't expect the game to end like this. The victorious wrestler was gasping and excitedly showing his bicep muscles to the public, giving expressions as if saying, 'Is there someone who could dare to fight me!' The pride of becoming a champion was visible on his face. To this, a farmer standing just behind Bhagban Chandra Bose boasted in a loud voice that this wrestler was getting impatient in vain, even he could beat this wrestler.

Bhagban Chandra Bose could hear this bragging. He looked back at the farmer and asked, 'Do you really want to fight?' When the farmer said 'Yes', Mr Bose held his hand, took him to the arena and got the winning wrestler hand-to-hand with the farmer.

Wrestling started and in a while, the farmer seemed strong and powerful. The farmer didn't just brag after all. The policeman started getting weak against him. After a few setbacks, his ego woke up—the policeman thought about his honour and he started blazing with the fire of revenge. Putting aside the rules of the game, he grabbed the farmer's throat between his legs, due to which the farmer got breathless and started fluttering.

The public started making noise but no one dared to go in front of the policeman wrestler. Jagadish was shocked to see the farmer fluttering. The wrestler choked the farmer. Bhagban Chandra Bose quickly reached the middle of the arena and ordered the policeman to release the farmer but he refused to obey even Bose's order. He still held the farmer's throat between his legs while the farmer was still flailing about. Saliva was dripping from his mouth.

Bhagban Chandra Bose quickly hit the police wrestler with his leg so hard that he groaned and loosened his grip on the farmer's neck. After hitting him once or twice more, he left the farmer and the arena in anger. By then, the farmer had fainted and he was brought to his senses by sprinkling water. There was a stir among the police personnel too and people started to disperse towards the fair.

In the evening, a *Jatra* (a religious procession) was organized at the fair. Earlier, the farmers used to play *Ram Katha* in a big tent along with the other cultural events. Bhagban Chandra Bose was supposed to join the cultural event which was to be held before the *Jatra*. Jagadish used to love watching the *Ram Katha* staged too.

The policeman, burning for revenge, reached the tent's door along with some of his colleagues. He started harassing the farmers who were coming to take part in the *Jatra*. Hearing the loud noises from the fight, someone ran and informed the Deputy Magistrate who was walking along and watching the fair. Bhagban Chandra Bose immediately reached there and ordered the police personnel to stand in attention posture. He also ordered the wrestlers to throw away the bamboo sticks in their hands.

All the soldiers threw away the sticks, but the wrestler who was defeated in wrestling refused to do so. As soon as police personnel tried to snatch the sticks from him on the orders of Bhagban Chandra Bose, a thin long sword came out of it. The defeated wrestler had hidden his sword in the bamboo stick. He had plotted to kill Bhagban Chandra Bose. Due to Mr Bose, his respect as a wrestler was lost. He was furious and decided to kill Mr Bose as soon as he got the opportunity. As the sword appeared, his wicked plan came to the fore. Other soldiers also caught hold of it and his sword was snatched. They were waiting for the order of the Deputy Magistrate to arrest him. The wrestler was stunned when his intention to kill the Deputy Magistrate was exposed. He thought that now he would be in jail and severely punished. His mind slipped from the Himalayas of ego and fell into the ocean of fear. He was sweating and fell at Bose's feet, apologizing. He confessed that he was waiting to kill the Deputy Magistrate. Bhagban Chandra Bose stood still for some time, and then with a calm face, he ordered the wrestler, 'Get up and go back to your duty.' This behaviour of Bose's melted the wrestler's heart. It is said that after that incident, the police wrestler changed entirely and remained a good person for the rest of his life. He kept on coming to Bose from time to time and kept him informed about the well-being of his family.

Jagadish Chandra Bose was growing up seeing all this. Jagadish liked to sit near the river flowing behind his house, trying to quench his increasing curiosity. One day, sitting near the river, a thought occurred to him—where does all the water in the river come from? Then, many questions started coming into his mind one by one. Why does river water flow? Sometimes it flowed so fast that it carried trees and houses along with it. Where does so much water go? His father had told him that so much water comes from the snow melting on the mountains which later goes into the sea. Jagadish asked again how so much water reaches the mountains. Pointing towards the clouds, Bhagban Chandra Bose said that they are caused by water vapour and are going to the Himalayas. Jagadish was surprised by this cycle. Then he asked his father, 'Where is the place where the rivers originate? Is it a large lake, the mouth of a cave, or something else?'

Jagadish's father did not have an answer to this, so he said, 'Son! I have never seen the place where a river originates, so I do not know the answer to your question.' Whenever Bhagban Chandra Bose could not answer Jagadish's questions, Jagadish was surprised. His father knew everything—from the clouds to the methods of catching criminals. But when he could not answer Jagadish, the son used to look at him in astonishment. Once, his father told him, 'Son! There are numerous exciting and essential questions whose answers are still unknown. If a question interests you, try to find out the answer yourself. On this pretext, many more people will be helped by your quest.' When the number of Jagadish's questions started increasing, his father started thinking about sending him to school.

Children learn much more from the behaviour of those around them than from the orations and explanations of people. One day, while returning from the playground, Jagadish saw a large group of people standing around a man who was screaming. A boy who used to play with him told Jagadish that a lion from the nearby forest was roaming around the village and he attacked a sheep of a shepherd and took away the sheep. The injured shepherd was being treated by a Hakim. Jagadish was getting angry at the lion but he could not do anything. Even though Jagadish was not timid in his childhood, he was terrified of the dark. One evening, out of fear of the darkness, he had to refuse something asked of him by his mother. His mother got angry at this and said that it was a cowardly attitude and that he will lose his father's respect with such a level of fear. This taunt ripped Jagadish deep inside. It was deeply ingrained in his mind. It was unacceptable for him to humiliate his father by being weak. After hearing that, he immediately got up from his place and fulfilled his mother's order. The father was a hero of the child's world. Jagadish grew up listening to the stories of his father's courage and bravery. He wanted to be like him.

At this time, he must have been about 5-6 years old. He had to prove that he was not weak. The next day, when he went to the nearby field to play, he asked his friend where the lion who had injured the shepherd the day before was hiding. His friend pointed to a sugarcane field far away from the playground and said that the lion had run towards that sugarcane field after picking up the sheep. Jagadish was still bleeding from his mother's remarks. Knowing about the lion, Jagadish returned home, took his father's *kukri* (a sharp knife) from the house, and left for the field.

He entered the sugarcane field with a *kukri*. It was tough to enter a sugarcane field. The long leaves of the sugarcane plants were sharp, which meant cuts on the body. In this field, the sugarcane was sown close to each other. There was no place to go beyond the canes. The village people knew that no matter how one enters the densely sown sugarcane field, it was complicated to come out. Once inside, one could see nothing beyond the tall sugarcane plants. The leaves rustled with the gust of wind and it now felt dreadful. Jagadish sometimes felt that someone was coming at him from the right and sometimes from the left. Seeing and hearing all this and thinking about it, he started to feel afraid. He was already scared. In his stubbornness, a person feels all the creepy caves of fear in the palace. Contumacy is a comparatively more intense emotion than fear. Jagadish had reached the sugarcane field riding on a violent bull of this stubbornness but it was becoming difficult for him to go further between the tall sugarcane plants. The sharp leaves of sugarcane peeled his hands and feet in many places. Riding on the rustle of leaves, fear was hovering around him. After reaching a long way inside the field, the fear in him started to overwhelm his senses. Then, a crow cawed, and now the dreadful claws of terror overtook his persistence. Jagadish became frightened and tried to get out of the field. In his panic, he forgot the way back.

The sugarcane field was dense and wherever Jagadish went, he could see a long forest of sugarcane in front of him. He got up and stood in one place, looking up. Then, as soon as he looked up and saw the sun, he remembered that his father had told him to guess the direction by looking at the sun, but he had never needed to guess the direction like this. On looking at the sun, he got an idea of where he had entered. After a while, he came out of the field. Jagadish was so afraid that he ran from there. The next moment, he was crying, clinging to his mother.

After a long time, when he returned to normal, he told his mother the whole story. Every mother in the world likes to see her son brave, but few mothers would have the courage to see their son crying. Jagadish's mother was very sorry that she had taunted her son. They were lucky that nothing untoward happened. Jagadish also realized from this incident that being brave and courageous is not as easy as it seems in his father's case. He had seen his father be calm in every situation and he had thought that everything in the world would be easy.

When his father came home, Jagadish had only one question for him, 'Dad, don't you feel afraid?' Dad simply smiled at this question and said lovingly, 'Son! Everyone feels fear. Fear must be overcome and it is necessary to know the circumstances. It is important to understand the strengths and weaknesses of both you and the other person.' When his mother told his father about fighting the lion with a knife, love for his child came into his eyes. He put his hand on Jagadish's head and said that he needed a strong brain more than a knife to fight! 'Learn to use your mind before you use knives.'

3

The Unconventional Mentorship

Jagadish had become quite playful now and he was full of energy. Jagadish's father now wanted to send him to school. He wanted the child's energy to be focused on the right things. Jagadish's questions increased day by day and it was now necessary for him to go to school anyway. At the time, he was around 5 years old. Children were not sent to school at such a young age at the time, but his father decided to send Jagadish because of his energy and curiosity.

At that time, there were only two schools in Faridpur. One was a government school, where English was taught and the other was a school that taught in the local language. The children of the rich and employed people of the town studied in the government school and the ordinary and poor people studied in the Bengali school. Bhagban Chandra Bose had set up a Bengali school for the education of the children of the district's poor, in which the children of shepherds, labourers and fishers used to study. Bhagban Chandra Bose considered education the most important thing. He was a fine scholar and an excellent example of the English-medium British education system. An English-medium government school was already established in Faridpur but the district's general public were hesitant about learning English. As a language, Bhagban Chandra Bose considered English as the language of his *Annadata,* or ruler. Because the tendency towards education had increased among the commoners' children, Bhagban Chandra Bose had opened a school in the town which taught in Bengali language. He was happy to see the children in his district getting educated. However, the condition of this school was poorer than the English-medium government school. Since it was a new school, resources were not ample.

When it was time to send Jagadish to school, everyone was astonished to hear that the Deputy Collector of Faridpur district, Bhagban Chandra Bose, had decided to send his only son to a local school imparting education in the Bengali language. A school where the children of fishers and labourers used to study. Even the children of the peons in the office of Bhagban Chandra Bose were studying in an English-medium school. Everyone seemed to be very surprised by this decision. There were rumours in the office that the collector wanted to show off by sending his only child to the local school. Bhagban Chandra Bose himself gave a lot of priority to his society and his people. The general public respected him and so many people were jealous of his aura. Those who could talk to him in the office tried to convince Bhagban Chandra Bose, 'Sir! Jagadish Babu will not be comfortable in a Bengali school. He should be sent to an English school only.' But no one dared ask him why he had decided to send Jagadish to the Bengali school.

Bhagban Chandra Bose's wife herself was not happy with him. She wanted to make her son a person of high status. For her, what her husband was doing was sacrificing their child for his social service and simplicity. She had made her intentions clear by telling her husband, 'You should keep aside our son's education from your social affairs. What will he learn if he studies with poor, illiterate children? Don't you want him to study well and achieve a high status, thus raising your fame?' Bhagban Chandra Bose tried to convince her that to become a successful person, Jagadish needed to know about his own language, culture and people.

Bhagban Chandra Bose believed that the child's primary education should be in his mother-tongue to understand his country and times better. He should understand his fellow people. If Jagadish was to become an administrator like his father, it was essential to understand his fellow people. He should not be proud of just his father's stature like many of the upper-class Indians. After many arguments, Jagadish's mother agreed to send her child to an ordinary school. But on the condition that if she felt that Jagadish's habits were deteriorating, she would send him to an English-medium school.

Thus, it was decided that Jagadish had to attend a Bengali-medium school for his primary education. According to that time, he was starting school early. His classmates were 2–3 years older than him. There were no chairs or tables available for students there like in English-medium school. All the students used to sit on the ground and had to carry a small cotton carpet with them to sit on. There was a big ground in front of the school where children used to play. Everyone brought food from home for lunch. Jagadish's tiffin was different from the rest of the children. The rest of the children did not have very expensive tiffins. They used to bring rice in bundles. Jagadish's father had taught him to share food with all of them. Everyone ate and played together.

Soon, Jagadish made several friends in school. He would eat food from different friends' houses every day. He ate new fish with a new taste every day—new stories to be heard every day. The lives of his friends' families were brand new to Jagadish and it was a new world with which Jagadish was unfamiliar. Coming from school in the evening, he would go to his house with his friends and play with them. The houses of his friends were tiny, many did not even have homes. They used to live in huts. The sons of the fishermen used to go catch fish to help their fathers. When they came to school the next day, he would have all the fishing stories and adventures.

Where do all these fish come from? Where does the water come from? Where does the river come from?

Jagadish started to feel like playing among questions and answers. He loved riding on the horse with his father. His mother was happy in her heart that her son was not a troubled child entangled in questions alone. His mind was also engaged in worldliness. She wanted her son to be brave and intelligent. She hoped that her son would become more courageous than his father, whose glory should be spread over the whole country and the world. However, she did not understand the plans of Jagadish's father regarding the future of the child. She preferred to remain calm in this regard and used to change the subject as soon as the conversation started on Jagadish's future. His mother believed in giving the necessary support. She encouraged Jagadish to jump into games. At the same time, she was cautious that Jagadish's studies and sports should be in harmony. She always told the child, 'Time is the most expensive commodity in the world, it is available to everyone in limited quantity and it should be used very thoughtfully.'

Once, Jagadish strongly insisted on riding a horse. His parents and all the servants in the house were busy with their own work. When the mother started feeling helpless, she became angry with Jagadish. When his father came home in the evening, Jagadish was sitting with his mouth shut. When his father asked the reason, his mother told the whole story. His father placed his hand on the son's shoulder and said, 'Son! Every favourite thing in life is not found immediately. Learn to be patient.' After that, he started telling interesting stories from his office to Jagadish. Jagadish usually loved listening to the adventurous stories of his father. His father had to solve issues by talking to different types of people in the office. Jagadish's mind was stuck on horse-riding that day, so he was not interested in office matters. Understanding Jagadish's mind, the father advised Jagadish, 'If you like horse-riding so much, why don't you learn to ride?' Jagadish's face lit up just like sunflowers bloom seeing the morning sun.

But the next moment, the boy felt that he was too young and his feet were too small to ride a horse. Jagadish became disheartened thinking of this. He asked Dad, 'Am I too young for horse-riding?' His father smiled and asked the child to be patient. The next day, a pony and a servant became regulars for Jagadish. The servant's job was to teach Jagadish to ride a pony. A horse would have been too tall for Jagadish, so he was given a pony. Jagadish's happiness knew no bounds. This pony was now his 'little horse'.

One day, he asked the horse-riding teacher about the difference between a pony and a horse. The master said that the pony is mainly for carrying goods and is not as fast as a horse. After understanding the difference between a pony and a horse, he wanted to ride only a horse. As soon as his father came to the house in the evening, he kept his point in front of him. He said that he was not a commodity that the pony would carry him from one place to another. All he needed was a horse for a ride. Dad said, 'Jagadish! It is just the beginning. The beginnings are not always perfect. It's okay to use the help of a pony to learn to ride. What matters is how well you learn to ride! If you learn to ride properly, whether you get a pony or a horse, you will enjoy the ride.'

He said, 'The question is not even where you started—it is only important where you ended.' His father also promised to give him a small horse after some time, but he said that he would have to learn to ride a pony well before that. Jagadish was satisfied with his father's promise and he was also anxious about the day when he would ride a horse. His father's words had such an effect on him that Jagadish would take his pony wherever he went. He loved the pony like a horse, helped it feed himself and bathed it. It was like a new friend to him.

Faridpur was a vibrant district. Jagadish's father used to organize different programmes in the city and encourage any cultural or sports events. In every programme in the community, people wanted to invite him as their guest. Once, at a horse-racing tournament to which he was invited, Jagadish requested to accompany him. Jagadish thought he should not go on his father's horse but his pony and father readily allowed it. In this way, Jagadish and his father, Bhagban Chandra Bose, reached to see the horse race.

Jagadish was roaming around on his pony. While turning, he reached where the horses were about to take part in the race. His mind was eager to talk to the horsemen. He was walking among the horses on his pony. Someone jokingly said to him, 'Your pony is wonderful—you should also take part in the race.' He had spoken what was on Jagadish's mind. He immediately went to his father and sought permission to participate in the race. Seeing Jagadish, Bhagban Chandra Bose laughed and looking at Jagadish, he thought a little while and then said, 'If you wish so, then go take part in the horse race.' Jagadish reached the seventh heaven for a moment but he became serious the next. The racetrack was long and his pony was much smaller than the other horses. Also, Jagadish did not know anything about the race. But now, he had to participate in the race or else everyone would laugh at him.

His pony was prepared for the race in a hurry. Jagadish participated in the race. In no time, he was running behind the other horses. He was repeatedly shouting to make the pony run faster. His pony soon gasped. But Jagadish did not lose his courage. His pony ran through the race. Jagadish was so lost in his enthusiasm, he did not realize that the sharp corners of a pedal were rubbing against his foot. By the time the race was over, he had a wound in his leg, and blood was dripping from it. After the race was over, he was taken to the doctor and bandaged.

The wound was so deep that its mark remained on his foot for the rest of his life. Jagadish Chandra Bose used to refresh the memories of his childhood days by showing wounds in his old age. This incident gives an idea of his character moulded during his childhood. His father's guidance was behind the bravery of Jagadish. Jagadish was timid at the beginning of his childhood, but he slowly evolved. There was another critical sequence of events behind this change.

It was when Jagadish was about to start school. One day Bhagban Chandra Bose was busy solving matters in the files sitting in his office. In the meantime, his clerk informed him that someone about 50 years old was waiting to see him. There was no dearth of people waiting for the Collector Bhagban Chandra Bose. It was a daily count that ten–twelve people came to him with their problems and returned after getting solutions.

This middle-aged man was a dreaded dacoit sentenced to rigorous imprisonment many years ago. He had looted the village many times and committed many murders. Although his behaviour had improved a lot in prison, he had lived too long in the prison system. Now, he was standing on the threshold of his old age. Bhagban Chandra Bose knew him. He had also helped in capturing some bandits. When the former dacoit entered his room to meet Bhagban Chandra Bose, he recognized him, asked him to sit down and congratulated him on his release from prison. Instead of being happy, the former dacoit became sad when complimented on his release. He said that it's good that he has been released from jail, but his family and society would not accept him. He was alone and his parents were dead. Since he was a well-known dacoit, no one would give him a job. His plea was that he was alone in this world and could not earn his bread outside of the jail, so he should be kept in prison till he dies. This way, he could live and also continue to be responsible for the jail's activities.

It was a bizarre request to a Deputy Collector. Everyone wants to come out of jail and live free, but he wanted to go back to jail for his whole life. He had spent so many years in prison that the prison seemed to have become his home. He feared the society as an animal of the forest is afraid of coming to the city. Bhagban Chandra Bose thought for a while and said, 'It is difficult to send you to jail again unless you commit a few more serious crimes. But I can arrange for your living. You can stay at my house from tomorrow. My child is about to start going to school. You will be responsible for transporting him to and from school.'

Shadows of comfort were seen on the man's face. He started taking Jagadish to school. It would take some time to reach school and during this time, Jagadish would walk with him listening to the stories of robberies. There were many scars on the man's body and Jagadish was profoundly interested in hearing the stories behind these scars. These stories had elements of bravery, plans for robbery, cohesion of the group, success and failures. Jagadish had found a friend in him. In the years of childhood, older people become the best friends. They have the stagnation of a deep ocean due to their experiences and the waves of their desires bounce on the shores of their memories. Jagadish used to spend a lot of time with this friend.

In the evening, both of them would go for a walk. The middle-aged man knew the forests very well—the river, the field, the barn, the paths, the trees and the plants. His youth was spent scouring these forests. He did not remember how often he had crossed the overflowing river swimming. There were tales of their bravery, of returning empty-handed from the robberies and of escaping by hiding and saving their lives somehow. The reformed dacoit significantly contributed to Jagadish's life and character building.

Once upon a time, Bhagban Chandra Bose and his family were going to their native village of Rarikhal in Bikrampur. There was a river on the way to the town. Transport at that time was based on water. Bhagban Chandra Bose was a little late in doing office work. It was getting late to reach home and it was getting dark. Jagadish was also going home with his father and mother. His caretaker friend accompanied Jagadish. Suddenly, they felt a boat was following them. There were many sailors in this boat and they were coming fast towards his boat. Then some other boats started to appear nearby. It meant that robbers had surrounded their boat. The robbers of the area were considered very ruthless and dreadful. There was no way to escape them. At that point, the middle-aged caretaker came to the side of the boat and he started giving some signals in a unique vocal tone. Hearing these signals, the boats turned back. Jagadish was very surprised at this. The former dacoit said, 'My voice gesture meant that a dacoits' family was travelling in this boat.' It was a code language of the dacoits.

Jagadish found this exciting. He kept thinking for many days about the signals sent in the coded language that saved his family's lives. Jagadish's family reached home safely, but new questions began to arise in Jagadish's mind. How are these secret signs formed? Who makes these? If the boat is far away, how will these signals reach the other party? That middle-aged man, the reformed dacoit, would answer Jagadish according to his intelligence and age. He was becoming Jagadish's hero.

Jagadish was pleased with the village visit. He walked a lot in the fields with his grandfather. Grandmother fed him different vegetables grown in the village and different types of fish were served.

After spending the holidays there, everyone came back to Faridpur. He resumed his old routine in Faridpur. He would go to school, study, play with his fisherman friends and come back with the reformed dacoit. They had a sports period at school in which they used to play games. Once, Jagadish's friends said that the children of the convent school were taught a strange game which the British played. Many people were playing with a ground ball and an oddly shaped long wood in this game. One throws the ball, and the other hits the ball with the wood. It was a strange 'British game' called cricket.

A boy from his class learned this game from the children of the convent school. Now the children of his class insisted that they also wanted to play cricket. His school did not have the money to buy expensive things like cricket bats and balls. These items were not even cheap enough to be purchased by saving the pocket money of all these boys. The children were frustrated and they found it a dream to play cricket.

One day, all the boys were sitting together and eating food. Among them, the father of a boy was a carpenter. All the children were talking amongst themselves—the issue was how to make a bat and a ball? Somebody suggested that the wood be cut and rubbed into a bat. A boy took over the work of getting good wood and another boy took up cutting and grinding wood. Now that the bat was to be made, the bigger question was how to make a ball? The ball made of cloth was very light, with the fabric wrapped outside by placing stones inside it, and the material kept falling open again and again. The kids weren't getting a suitable ball. When Jagadish returned from school, he would go for a walk in the forest on the way. The former dacoit would show Jagadish unique plants and trees. One day, he showed Jagadish a tree from which a strange substance came out which people used to stick things with. It dried up and became soft. It was a rubber tree, whose trunk when scraped with a knife produced a rubbery substance. It would become soft and light by drying, whatever form it was cast in. It was neither too light nor too heavy and stiff.

Jagadish jumped with joy after seeing this. He had found a way to make balls for his friends. During the holidays, Jagadish along with the dacoit and his friends brought a lot of rubber out of the trees and made a rubber ball. Coconuts were used as the moulds. A few days later, the children of the government school were also playing cricket. And the most beautiful thing about this incident was that they made the ball and the bat with their own hands. One can call it Jagadish's first step in his long journey of innovativeness.

The reformed dacoit stayed with Jagadish's family till Jagadish's father was transferred to another district. For about four or five years, Jagadish received support from him. Later, his father was transferred to the Bardhaman district. This caretaker wanted to come with Jagadish's father to Bardhaman but Jagadish's father advised him to stay there. In these four-five years, he gained a good name and also had the tag of working in the house of Collector Sahib. A life of honour was now waiting for him. With the help of Bhagban Chandra Bose, he built a small house and started living his life smoothly. Whenever Bhagban Chandra Bose came to Faridpur district for some work, he would meet this man and was satisfied to see him happy. Such officers are still rare who can believe on their reforms and the reformed criminals in this way.

4

Tryst with Karna

Bhagban Chandra Bose became busier with time. Jagadish's curiosity also kept growing parallel to his father's busyness. As he mingled with the outside world, the number of his questions kept increasing. He was amazed by whatever he saw in the world. In childhood, we all marvel at the incredible structure of nature, some less, some more. The most important thing is that after being surprised, we should get correct answers. We all tend to ask questions out of curiosity but most of us get wrong answers in return for our inquiries. No one tells us that they don't know the answer. Jagadish's father's response was often this, 'Perhaps no one knows the answer to this question—you should try to find out yourself.' Jagadish was constantly surprised by this answer and asked his father again, 'Is it even possible? I am so young right now and I don't understand anything. How will I find the answers to questions that no one knows?' Bhagban Chandra Bose used to reply, 'Son! Finding answers to these questions is not a single day's task. But man is the only creature on earth that aspires to discover the laws of nature. Because he wishes, he finds. If you start taking your questions seriously today, you will have answers to many difficult questions to tell your children by my age.'

Jagadish just nodded his head in response. Perhaps he felt himself standing at the edge of the journey of a lifetime. The best father would be the one whose sons/daughters are like his friends. Those who teach children to see the world through their own eyes. Often, parents get busy with their work. The structure of our society at that time was also such that there was very little communication between fathers and sons. Children usually grew up trying to remain polite and cultured in front of their mothers. Mothers were often the emotional support of children, but rarely did they become good friends to their children. That was not the case with Jagadish. Whenever his father came home after retiring from the district's problems, he would lie next to Jagadish till he was done talking. Since Jagadish felt that his father was the best to answer his questions, he would wait for his father to come. Many times, it would be late at night.

Bhagban Chandra Bose had immense love for the people of his district. He always strived for the development of the community. He wanted the economic well-being of his people as well as their social and cultural development. Along with being progressive, he also had deep faith in Indian culture. Despite being very busy in administrative activities, he used to find time for cultural programs in the district. He started organizing a fair in Faridpur which continued to be held every year. He greatly encouraged religious festivals and traditional arts. He also created an exhibition for farmers and local manufacturers/traders. In this exhibition, farmers used to display a variety of products. Local merchants used to display new products which were made for the farmers and the general public.

All of this was a big deal for the nineteenth century East Bengal. Various types of games were organized for the local players. Jagadish Chandra Bose would tell all this later, remembering his childhood days. He also had fresh memories of *Jatra*. In *Jatra*, the artists travelled from one place to another on chariots performing the events of the Indian epics and people would gather around to watch them. These trips were very well-liked not only by the local people but also by the British. Once, an English Chief Magistrate came to a fair and watched the performances of the artists. He was so happy that he emptied his pockets distributing money among those artists. He was still not satisfied with this; he went home apologizing and got a lot of money and gifts that were given to the artists.

These cultural programs had left a profound impact on Jagadish. He was so fascinated by these epics that he started to mimic the characters in his daily life. Dad told him that there were many such epics that were written countless years ago. Jagadish was astonished to know this. As he learned to read, his father brought him *Puranas* and epics like *The Ramayana* and *The Mahabharata*. Jagadish read them with great fervour. The habit of reading books was inculcated in him from a young age which later gave a new dimension to Jagadish's personality. As a child, he liked the characters of Ram and Lakshman. But these characters were probably too ideal. The characters of *Mahabharata*, meanwhile, had all the demerits, shortcomings and flaws like humans. They behaved like great humans in one moment and they would become weak in the next. Jagadish felt closer to these characters. He liked the character of Karna in *Mahabharata* very much. Karna eventually became his childhood hero. Jagadish would have been 9-10 years old then. He could not let go of that character till his death. Till the end of his life, he used to remember Karna's statements in the play which he used to repeat with great pleasure. He drowned in them and narrated the tales of Karna throughout his life.

Karna's mother had left him on the river banks when he was a newborn. He was picked up by a charioteer's wife who brought him up. The charioteer taught him archery. Karna became so proficient in archery that his name began to be discussed among the then greats. Tales of his greatness began to be told. But being a member of the lower caste of chariot drivers, he was always humiliated. Then, the Kauravas gifted him a small princely state, impressed by his bravery. It was a big deal for Karna. He became the admirer and benefactor of the Kauravas.

Karna fought several wars for the Kauravas. Duryodhana, the prince of Hastinapur, treated Karna like his best friend. He treated Karna as an equal, whom the entire society had rejected and humiliated for belonging to a low caste despite being unparalleled in archery. In the words of Jagadish himself, 'Karna was the eldest brother among the Pandavas. According to the rules, Karna should have been the king. When Arjuna was welcomed everywhere with grandeur, Karna arrived like a stranger.' In response to Arjuna asking Karna to introduce himself, Karna's words were important, and Jagadish Chandra Bose used to narrate those like this, 'I am my own ancestor. Just as you don't ask Mother Ganga of her source, her flow itself is her identity. In the same way, my karma is mine alone.'

Karna was abandoned everywhere but he never gave up. He always fought ethically. It was not Karna's intention to be immoral even on the question of life and death in war. When Karna became a threat to Arjuna's life in battle, Lord Krishna realized that Karna was more skilled than Arjuna in archery. Arjuna would not be able to win over Karna, so he convinced Arjuna's mother, Kunti, to go to Karna and say that he was Kunti's son. She had given birth to Karna before marriage. They thought that Karna, accepting this, would leave the Kauravas and join the Pandava clan with Arjuna. But upon hearing this, Karna replied 'No' to Kunti. Karna said that those who brought him up were his parents. Duryodhana respected his learning, so he will always consider Duryodhana as his king. But he gave a promise to Kunti that he would not harm any of the Pandavas except Arjuna. His war was with Arjuna's archery.

Despite this, Kunti asked him to donate the *Kavach-Kundal* (blessed protective armours). Karna happily donated those, knowing that *Kavach* and *Kundal* were the saviours of his life. No one could shake Karna's character. Arjuna was to be killed by a single arrow of Karna on the battlefield, but Lord Krishna himself was sitting on Arjuna's chariot. In front of Arjuna, Lord Krishna was present as a protector. According to the epics, as soon as Karna shot the arrow, Lord Krishna shook the earth a little and the arrow only shortened Arjuna's hair. But that magic arrow was made only to kill Arjuna, so it turned around and came back in the hands of Karna and said, 'I am made only to kill Arjuna. Great Karna, fire me again!' Karna did not know this. Hearing this from the arrow, Karna did not shoot that arrow again. Karna wanted to kill Arjuna with his skill and not with the power of the mighty magical arrow. This time, when Karna was about to shoot the second arrow, Lord Krishna, seeing the danger, made a crack in the ground under Karna's chariot, due to which a wheel of the chariot got stuck in the ground. As soon as Karna got down from the chariot and bent to remove the chariot's wheel, Lord Krishna ordered Arjuna to shoot an arrow at Karna. It was against war ethics, but Arjuna killed Karna while he was unarmed at the behest of Lord Krishna. Karna kept fighting till the end. Even if the gods were against him and fighting unethically, Karna was firm as ever. He fought strategically and ethically till his death and was killed in the end. This bravery was higher and far more extraordinary than the victory of Arjuna.

Later, Jagadish used to remember the same of his father, 'I love my father as a similar hero. He always struggled for the upliftment of his people, even if he was not so successful and got back very little. It also taught me to see through visible success. Victory or success is too meaningless, while conflicts, struggles and defeats are far greater. True success comes only through failures. It is one of the greatest teachings that war should be ethical and clear.

Victory should never be achieved on false principles. Its path should be clear and straight, no matter how difficult the road.' Jagadish Chandra Bose often told these words to his disciples and students. These principles also shaped his life.

Bhagban Chandra Bose was transferred from Faridpur district in 1869 and he was promoted as the Assistant Commissioner of Bardhaman district of Bengal. At that time, Jagadish was 11 years old. Bhagban Chandra Bose stayed in Bardhaman till 1874. There was not much office work for him in Bardhaman. It used to be a vacation spot for the residents of Calcutta at that time. People used to come here for mental relaxation and well-being. Bardhaman is an old and historical city of Bengal. Its history is believed to have started from 5000 BC. In the sixth century BC, it was called Bardhaman after the twenty-fourth Tirthankara of Jainism, 'Mahavir'. According to Jainism's religious text *Kalpasutra*, Lord Bardhaman had spent some time of his life here. At that time, its name was *Aastikgram*. Later, the Mughal emperor Jahangir changed its name to *Badh-e-Diwan*. This city has been the headquarters of the Maharaja of Bardhaman.

The history about the kings of Bardhaman is also important. The Hindu Khatri Raja Sangam Rai founded Bardhaman Raj in Lahore (now Pakistan). The kings of his generations first served the Mughals and then the British Raj. In 1855, due to the efforts of Maharaja Mahtab Chand who was loyal to the British, rail transport started from Howrah to Bardhaman. In 1868, pleased with his loyalty to the British, the British gave Maharaja Mahtab Chand a 'state-mark' and a large amount of money along with it. In the Santhal rebellion and the first armed rebellion of 1857, Mahtab Chand supported the British and put his life at stake for them. Later in 1877, the British permitted Maharaja Mahtab Chand to take the thirteen-gun salute.

The efforts of Maharaja Mahtab Chand for the cultural, educational and economic development of Bardhaman cannot be ignored. There was Bardhaman Raj College in Bardhaman whose financial expenditure was looked after by Bardhaman Kingdom. The land's educational and cultural climate gave birth to many Bengali poets, including Pratap Chand Roy who published an English translation of *The Mahabharata* at the same time (1883–96).

Tourism was also flourishing in Bardhaman. Although the then Assistant Commissioner's administrative responsibilities were limited, Bhagban Chandra Bose became active as soon as he came to Bardhaman. At that time, people were scientifically unaware of the malaria disease. Malaria took the form of an epidemic in Bengal around 1870. Thousands of people died in this epidemic that started in 1870. Countless children became orphans, women widowed and old parents were left alone. Relief work began in full swing in the Bardhaman district. Bhagban Chandra Bose came forward in the administrative relief work and took up the responsibility. He believed that this disaster could not be overcome by simply distributing relief material. The epidemic had assumed a formidable form in four years. It considerably impacted the economy of the district.

Bhagban Chandra Bose was thinking about the next ten years. He started promoting the establishment of small-scale industries. Along with that, efforts were also made to train the youth to work in these industries. He wanted the disaster-stricken youth to find their own employment opportunities and be trained for them. Plans were made to set up small-scale industries and to start training the youth, but there was no place to start the training program. The residential bungalow of Bhagban Chandra Bose in Bardhaman was very spacious. He decided that half of his residential bungalow would be vacated for the Industrial Training Institute.

In this way, the training of unemployed youth started. All the equipment were arranged there. There was a carpentry system for woodworking and a metallurgy system to make tools by melting metals and pouring them into moulds. The young generation got busy making their future. A copper pot and an heirloom made in this metallic foundry are still kept in Bose's home in Calcutta. Even after 150 years, the lustre of the copper of this pot is proof that the people of Bardhaman had become proficient in these works. Jagadish watched all of this work being done in his house. He would sit near the artisans for hours and learn. One day, Jagadish told his father that the British had provided good weapons to the king of Bardhaman. His father was very appreciative of the quality of those weapons. An idea came to Jagadish's mind whether he could make a gun on his own. His father said that it could be made in a foundry but Jagadish will have to take the help of the artisans of the foundry.

One day, Jagadish took some old utensils and other useless copper items from his mother and reached the foundry. From that copper, Jagadish made a regular-size cannon with the help of the artisans. He used this cannon to fire from time to time for fun. Everyone is fond of toys, but the enthusiasm for making toys is something higher. Jagadish kept this cannon for a long time. For Jagadish, the excitement of making scientific toys started with this cannon and lasted a lifetime. He kept making scientific toys for himself throughout his life.

Bhagban Chandra Bose felt encouraged by the success of his efforts to increase employment opportunities. He knew that economic upliftment of the society was needed at an urgent basis. However, the efforts for cultural and political developments are not priorities over economic growth. When people do not have enough food to eat and clothes to wear, why would they read literature, take out *Jatra* and sing songs? Bhagban Chandra Bose intensified his efforts for economic reforms. In the meantime, he was transferred again. It was the year 1875 when he was appointed executive officer-in-charge and sent to the Katwa sub-division.

One of Jagadish's father's biggest concerns at the time was sending Jagadish to a good school. Bardhaman's schools were not enough for Jagadish, so Bhagban Chandra Bose sent him to Calcutta for further studies. Jagadish got enrolled in Hare School, Calcutta. Here, studies were in English-medium although the children used to talk in Bengali. For Jagadish, it was like coming to another planet. He spoke to the teachers in broken English but it was a challenging task for him every time. Jagadish stayed at Hare School for three months. After this short transition, his father enrolled him in St Xavier's School, the best-reputed school in Calcutta.

After studying among the children of fishermen and labourers, Jagadish was in a school where children of senior British officers were studying. One can try to understand how a Bangla vernacular-speaking child would feel among English-speaking children and teachers. Faridpur may have been a township but its atmosphere was largely rural. Jagadish's father was a very down-to-earth and straightforward person, so at home there was no sense of the elite. Jagadish had started making a place in Hare School. But he did not know that Hare School was just a small exercise in the struggle to survive at St Xavier's School.

Those three months made Jagadish sorely hopeful that a boy from the village would be saved from getting lost in the glare of Calcutta. The most challenging part was that Jagadish did not have his family with him. He was staying in a hostel. There was no one far and wide so that this small 9-year-old child could ease his mind by narrating his agony. At that time, there were neither mobile phones nor wireless systems. Letters were the only support of the people who lived far away. And this young child was not a writer who knew how to write down his sorrows in letters to his parents. Days passed. Jagadish was stubborn. His father and his dacoit uncle never taught him to back down. At night, he would dream of Karna who taught him that even if Gods stood against him, he should neither give up nor back down.

St Xavier's School was originally established for the children of British officers to get a high-quality education. The children of a few Indian officers also studied in this school, though nominal in numbers. Jagadish could not make friends even in class. How would he talk to the English boys? In this way, his position in the class was also bizarre. Other children would make fun of him, thinking of him as mean and low. They would trouble Jagadish with their mischievous activities. He became a joke for everyone in the class. Someone would slap him from behind and run away, some other would secretly fill his bag with garbage. Jagadish was highly respected in the Faridpur school. Everyone wanted to talk to him and every boy wanted to be his friend. He didn't remember how many times he had gone to someone else's house and ate the tastiest food. He also did not misbehave with anybody in the class. And today, the British boys were troubling him by thinking of him as a village boy. Jagadish wished to leave Calcutta and go back to his father but it was not actually possible.

For a long time, the tinkering of other boys with Jagadish continued. Though he did not understand much, he would come home and work on his language. Little had he known that one day the British would become so important in his life, that he would have to struggle so much with them at school and with their English at home.

One day as soon as a teacher left the class for lunch, a boy threw pieces of paper into Jagadish's food. It was by chance that Jagadish saw him throwing it. Jagadish was already angry with their behaviour. He protested angrily and said that he was going to complain to the teacher. Then, a scuffle broke out between the students.

The boy was much stronger than Jagadish and thrashed him a lot. Jagadish's nose started bleeding, but the boy still didn't stop. While getting punched and kicked, the dacoit uncle and the tales he had narrated flashed in his mind for a moment. Suddenly,

Jagadish felt a lion awaken inside him. Jagadish was a child of the village who had inner strength; he had become weak only due to an inferiority complex in front of the British. In an instant, Jagadish swooped in and the white boy was below him.

Jagadish's long pent-up anger and frustration erupted on that classmate—he took his revenge by harshly beating his opponent. After the scuffle, the condition of the white boy was not good. He had to be treated medically. Jagadish's nose was also bleeding and was treated. After this, the class-teacher gave a long lecture to both of them. Both had to apologize. After serving a sentence together, the two became friends. The effect of fighting and beating up the most wicked boy in the class was that all the other children became soft with Jagadish and started respecting him. After this incident, his school life became a little easier. The wickedness of the boys stopped and no one dared to mess with Jagadish anymore in the class, but Jagadish still had to prove himself in his studies. English was still Jagadish's problem, as Bengali was of the British. Since the medium in the school was English, Jagadish did not want to give any chance to the children of the class to laugh at him. He did not talk to anyone in school, resorting to the least words if necessary.

Incidentally, the condition of his hostel was more or less the same. There was no hostel in his school since most of the children were of British officers and their families lived in Calcutta. In the hostel where Jagadish lived, boys were much older than him. Usually, those senior boys did not have time for this little boy. Jagadish himself preferred solitude and had nothing to talk about with those boys. When he came from school, he would be busy with English and the work assigned to him in school. After a few days, many of the boys felt that this child liked solitude, so even the one or two boys who used to take a look while leaving their room also stopped paying attention to him.

After a few months, Jagadish overcame the problem of language at school. The boys also helped him to a great extent.

Now, Jagadish felt the need for a friend. All the conversations with the boys in school were confined to the school and not outside. Jagadish felt very lonely in the hostel room but he could not find anyone to be friends with. It was very difficult to find boys who he could connect with.

In the meantime, Jagadish bought a parrot. Then, after the parrot, several other members were invited to Jagadish's room one by one. The pocket money received from his house was used to buy pet birds and animals and maintain them. Some plants were planted in a part of the hostel's courtyard which Jagadish used to call his garden. Slowly, the tiny garden started getting bigger. The boy got so busy that the feeling of needing friends stopped. Jagadish also planted the Lajjavati (*mimosa pudica*) plant in this garden which he had seen with his grandfather in his childhood. There were, of course, some beautiful plants and flowers in his garden, but not many plants behaved strangely like Lajjavati which would be seen in various ways from time to time. The behaviour of the plants was observed sometimes by adding less water, sometimes by adding more, by manure, by sunlight, or for other reasons.

'Look at this plant. When it feels a little thirsty, it drinks more water. That is a delicate plant like the British and withers in the sun. Look at it, touch it a little and then it becomes like this, like how a small child shrinks due to tickling.' This is how Jagadish would introduce people to the plants in his small, so-called garden. There was a gleam in Jagadish's eyes when he would say all this. Now, he was happy. There was a time when there was no one to talk to and now he had a garden of friends and a small zoo in the room. It was a pleasure for his father to see Jagadish's interest in nature but his mother found it a waste of time. She thought Jagadish should play and study more. But his father's consent was enough to take his interests forward.

Time flew by. When his pocket money increased, a unique piping system was designed and arranged to supply water to the hostel garden. After much brainstorming, it was decided that the thickness of the tubes should be determined according to how much water the plants need on each side. Now, giving water by taking a bucket from the tap was an old system. The garden was getting modern. Water would go through a giant pipe from the tap and at the right places, it would drip through the pipelines hidden in the soil. When Dad came the next time, he was shown this technique with great joy and enthusiasm. This childhood hobby remained with Jagadish till the last stage of his age. A similar pipeline was laid to water the plants in the garden of his residential house of Bose Institute much later. Jagadish Chandra Bose did not forget to talk about the pipelines hidden inside the soil when people visited his home while mentioning the plants. However, the design of those pipelines had become much better since his childhood.

When he had to go home during the summer vacations, Jagadish would spend most of his time pursuing his old hobbies. Horse-riding was one of them. Meanwhile, another place became very important for Jagadish. That place was the foundry, built by Bhagban Chandra Bose, which was half of the bungalow of Bardhaman. Jagadish's summer vacations were mostly spent in this part of the bungalow. He needed specially designed accessories for his zoo and sometimes a special pen to decorate his table. He would be busy making new kinds of designs for it. When Jagadish remembered his childhood, he would surely mention Bardhaman and Katwa.

5

Physics and the Father

In 1875, at the age of only 16, Jagadish graduated from school.

After schooling, it is often difficult to decide the way forward. Jagadish and his parents also had a similar dilemma; although at that time, there were not as many options as today. Even though Bengal has been at the forefront of India during the renaissance, in Jagadish's time, Bengal used to have only two colleges for higher education in science.

The story of the beginning of higher education in Bengal is no less interesting. By 1857, a large part of India was under the control of the British. The British had made presidencies in Calcutta, Madras, Bombay and Allahabad to rule such a vast area. Delhi was ruled by the British. They brought the systematic modern education system to India. Before the arrival of the British, there was no organized system of modern education in India around the sixteenth century on modern subjects like science. However, people continued their efforts at an individual level. Due to a strong caste system, not every section of the society got the chance to connect with knowledge. Acharya P.C. Ray, the great chemist of modern India, believed that the decay and distortion of the ancient knowledge of India was due to this system in which one class had the monopoly on knowledge. Raja Ram Mohan Roy significantly contributed to bringing the modern education system to India. Apart from Ram Mohan Roy, great personalities like Alexander Duff, David Hare and William Carey also worked tirelessly to bring the modern education system to India. However, the British officers of higher ranks wanted English education in India only to help them rule. The first educational institution was opened in Calcutta by the East India Company in 1780. Its name was Calcutta Mohammedan College in which English was taught at the formal level. The Asiatic Society was formed in 1781 by the efforts of Sir William Jones, who then established the Sanskrit College in Varanasi in 1793. In 1813, the British Parliament, renewing the charter of the East India Company, announced a budget of one lakh rupees for spreading knowledge and educating the people in the parts of British-ruled India. The maximum amount of this budget was spent on spreading the traditional knowledge of India.

Angered by this, Raja Ram Mohan Roy wrote a scathing letter to Lord Amherst in 1823. In this letter, he emphasized the need to increase the financial budget to pay special attention on teaching subjects like Chemistry, Natural Science and Physiology. Raja Ram Mohan Roy reminded Lord Amherst that the government is responsible for the educational development of these subjects. Dwarkanath Tagore, the grandfather of Rabindranath Tagore, also supported the views of Ram Mohan Roy. In 1817, Raja Ram Mohan Roy, Dwarkanath Tagore, the renowned educationist David Hare and some others founded the Hindu College in Calcutta, which was later renamed Presidency College in 1855.

Lord Amherst left India in 1828. After that, William Bentinck became the new viceroy who acted on the advice of Macaulay. Macaulay's ideas were not in favour of giving better education to the Indian people. Macaulay wanted to provide only as much education in India as needed, so that the British rule continued smoothly and Indians could not revolt. However, many Englishmen were liberal and wanted Indian students to be given equal opportunities alongside the British. Due to the efforts of all the scholars and social workers of Bengal, it was possible to establish the first medical school in Calcutta in 1835. It was an important event related to India's education-initiation of modern knowledge and science.

Meanwhile, the need for universities in India was beginning to be felt. The area of the British Indian colony was vast and surprisingly diverse, even at the cultural and geographical levels. The famous British officer, Sir Charles Wood, believed that if the people of India were educated, then with the help of reliable people among them, governance and administration could be done easily over India. However, he was afraid that the Indians might become a threat to the British by studying modern education. Charles Wood also harboured a lot of prejudice about Bengal. When Lord Dalhousie proposed the establishment of three universities in India to Wood, he agreed to establish universities in Madras and Bombay. But he did not want a university to be established in Bengal. He wrote in a letter to Dalhousie, 'It is great if they want to educate them, but I am against giving higher education to my future adversaries, rebels and complainers.' Dalhousie did not completely agree with Sir Charles Wood. Dalhousie's efforts are responsible for the establishment of Calcutta University in Bengal on 24 January 1857. Dalhousie also started many fellowships in India.

It took a long time for the British to change their attitude towards higher education in India and this happened very slowly. The reason behind this change could be the insistence of a few liberal British officials and the continuous demands of a few Indians. There was a massive lack of financial budget in the field of education. The distribution of the budget was also very uneven. At that time, the financial assistance to two colleges in Calcutta was at its maximum. One was Hindu College, now known as Presidency College, and the other was St Xavier's College. These two colleges were completely government-funded. All the professors here were English. In 1866, a modern physics laboratory was built in St Xavier's College, which was looked after by Father Lafont. Father Lafont used to be a famous teacher at that time in Bengal. He had inspired all of the students who were pursuing higher education in Physics at the time.

Father Lafont has made a significant contribution to Science education in Bengal. The students' interest in physics arose because of Father Lafont and he gave them the right direction for their interest. He is called the 'Father of Science in Bengal'. He came to India at the end of 1865. As soon as he arrived, he started his job as a Professor of Physics at St Xavier's College. Being a great teacher, he observed that even the best colleges in India do not have good laboratories. He believed that the teaching of science was incomplete without modern laboratories. Due to his efforts, a state-of-the-art laboratory was established in 1866. Father Lafont started a series of speeches that focused on scientific topics. The remarkable point is that he used to present scientific materials to the general public in these speeches. In between speeches, he would also show many experiments. Due to the simplicity and excellence of his speeches, the lecture hall used to be crowded with the general public. People used to listen to his lectures in the rain and in the lightning.

With the assistance of Alexander Pedler (the then Professor of Chemistry at Presidency College), Dr Mahendra Lal Sircar (who founded the Indian Association for the Cultivation of Science in 1876) and some people from the University of Calcutta, Father Lafont divided the degree of BA into two streams in 1872. Of these two streams, stream 'A' was purely literary and mathematics was kept in stream 'B'. It was a necessary and revolutionary step at that time. The students were taught inorganic chemistry, mathematics and geography in course 'B'. English was a compulsory subject and one had to choose among physics, geophysics and botany as an option. Meritorious students often opted for the course 'B'. Such a trend became customary in those days. Father Lafont was one of the reasons for this happening.

When Jagadish enrolled for higher education at St Xavier's College in 1875, Father Lafont was the rector (registrar) of the college and by now, his fame had spread to Calcutta. Jagadish had also opted for a science course. During his BA studies, Jagadish remained an average student. Jagadish learned a lot during his degree. College days are crucial in any person's life because the person learns about the world in a slightly broader scope. Universities don't teach just bookish knowledge—students become familiar with the realities of life there. The mist of uncertainty about the future, which was on their minds, gradually dissipated during this time. At the time of graduation, due to Father Lafont, Jagadish's interest in physics became very clear, although at that time it was only an optional course for him. Father Lafont used to demonstrate theory as well as experiments in the classroom. He used to arrange all of those experiments himself to make the subject exciting to students and experiments are always essential resources. With this, the students themselves learned to use the experimentation tools to understand nature with the help of the available resources. Dalton's atomic theory, taught by Prof. Lafont, became very popular among the students. Father Lafont's theoretical understanding and efficient teaching were such that all the students began to dream of becoming like him. One of those students was Jagadish Chandra Bose. Jagadish Chandra Bose wanted to be a better teacher than Father Lafont and to design scientific experiments even better than him.

Meanwhile, Jagadish Chandra Bose's father was transferred as the executive officer-in-charge of the Katwa subdivision in 1875. Katwa was going through a bad time. It was at a time when famine was spreading in Katwa. This famine remained at its peak till 1880. It was the most challenging disaster of Bhagban Chandra Bose's life and he tried hard to provide all possible government help to the people of his district during this disaster. Bhagban Chandra Bose was a compassionate person. He would leave the house early in the morning and engage in rescue work. He would reach home late at night. It was a huge task to organize massive assistance from British officials and get it to the general public. He kept working throughout the day. Seeing people suffering from hunger, his mind often got upset and he could not eat food. He also had a child in the house, studying at a high-order college in Bengal. When he saw the children of the villages suffering from starvation, his heart groaned with pain. Mr Bose would often distribute the food he took for his own lunch. It went on for a long time. The strenuous physical exertion and intense mental anguish had a profound effect on the physical health of Bhagban Chandra Bose. He became frail and started getting sick. Mr Bose's physical condition became so bad that his senior officers advised him to go on medical leave.

Bhagban Chandra Bose would often come to Calcutta on medical leave to spend time with Jagadish. He had a special attachment to Jagadish. Unfortunately, the Bose family had to face another accident in the meantime. Jagadish also had a younger brother who was living with the family. When Jagadish joined St Xavier's College, Calcutta, his brother was ten years old. He died suddenly in 1875. After his death, Jagadish's mother was very depressed. His father was engaged in saving his district from famine. He used to engage his mind by serving the children outside, but what could the mother do? After coming home late at night, Bhagban Chandra Bose would go to sleep exhausted, wake up early in the morning and leave again. A silence created by sadness had taken over the house. After arriving at the Katwa subdivision, the family's happiness went away. As soon as Bhagban

Chandra Bose got some relief, he started coming to Calcutta to meet his elder son, Jagadish. His medical leave lasted two years. In the meantime, he would come to Calcutta to meet his child, but his mind would be elsewhere. He was always thinking about the people of his famine-hit areas. He believed that the development of Bengal was impossible without the development of agriculture and industry. Whatever he was able to do with the government's help, he would do it, but at the same time, he used to spend his savings. It was not easy to get a lot of financial support from the British government for public welfare programs.

Meanwhile, he bought land in the Terai region. On this land, he started cooperative farming. The area's labourers and small farmers became partners in this collective farming. After a year of hard work, a good quantity of products started to come from this land. But due to this land being too far from any market, the sale of crop products could not be adequately made and thus, they suffered a lot. The farmers and labourers contributed their labour and Bhagban Chandra Bose invested money in this enterprise. For several reasons, it didn't work out. This effort to improve the economic condition of the people had to be stopped due to heavy losses.

Jagadish's father, Bhagban Chandra Bose, was a determined person as well. After some time, he again collected a few thousand acres of land in Assam with the help of his friends and acquaintances. This land was cleared to make it suitable for growing crops. This land was made clean after a lot of hard work and expenses and that was how it became a farm. Bhagban Chandra Bose intended to cultivate tea on this land. He used to think that if the people of Scotland could improve their living standards by growing good crops in difficult circumstances, why couldn't we Indians? The cost of making the land in Assam suitable for tea cultivation was much higher than Bose's initial estimate. To meet this expense, he had to take on a lot of debt.

Since this loan had to be taken suddenly, the rate of interest on the loan was very high. At that time, the conditions in Assam were not so good for agriculture and trade. Tea cultivation was started, but it was impossible to make enough profit to pay off the old loan's interest. It took years to get a profit from those tea gardens. After many years, things got a little better but the loans taken from many people were still pending.

When tea cultivation started in Assam, Bhagban Chandra Bose also started a Khadi weaving company in Bombay with the money left over from his last savings. All this came from his love for his own family and his people. In the country where there were movements for independence, the seeds of renaissance were being sown in Bengal. Bhagban Chandra Bose was worried about the economic condition of the country. He dreamt of a prosperous India. Mr Bose was full of hope and was happy to struggle for it. He invested on behalf of his partners in this weaving company, starting in Bombay. It was out of patriotism, to increase the self-reliance of his people. But later, this company also failed and closed down. Mr Bose had put all his remaining resources and deposits into this company. The reason for the closure of this company was that the members of the board of directors of this company, i.e., Bose's partners, disappeared after taking the money and could not be traced later. Bhagban Chandra Bose, having spent everything amid all these worries and burdened by heavy debt, tried to make his efforts successful even in his sick condition. He kept assuring the farmers and the workers of the tea plantation that their hard work would bring a significant change one day. But in the state of illness, his body could not bear so many worries and hard work. Another tragedy occurred during this time. His body became partially paralyzed. It took him a long time to recover from this paralysis, but all the calamities could not dominate him for long due to his confidence and determination. Even though all the misfortunes together did ruin him financially and physically, they could not defeat the mental strength and conviction of Bhagban Chandra Bose.

People often forget those who fail while fighting for a big social cause, even if they have sacrificed everything in this struggle, even if their intentions were steelier than those who succeeded later. We, as a public, find it easy to associate a brand with every major goal. Don't you smell the fragrance of a Swadeshi movement in these efforts of Bhagban Chandra Bose although it was not against British, which may have failed miserably but was equally rebellious in intent?

In the meantime, Jagadish completed his BA degree. In 1879, he got his BA degree from St Xavier's College, University of Calcutta, with a second division. Now, a more important question had come before him. Jagadish wanted to further his studies but he also wanted to support his father's struggle. Jagadish wanted to take care of his family's wellness, which was shattered to an extent.

6

Civil Services *vs* Science

After completing his BA degree from St Xavier's College, Jagadish Chandra Bose was conflicted about what path he should choose next. The company of Father Lafont had instilled a fascination for physics in him. Somewhere in his heart was buried the desire to study science. Bhagban Chandra Bose wanted him to go abroad and get a higher education in science. But seeing the circumstances of his house, he decided to do something to help his father get out of debt. One option he had was that he, like his father, could receive training in the Indian Civil Service. Neither did his father have money left to send him abroad to get a long-term higher education in science, nor did Jagadish have such good marks in BA Therefore, Jagadish finally made up his mind about Indian Civil Service training.

However, Jagadish's father had a different view on this. He did not want Jagadish to become an officer in the Indian Civil Services. Being an officer himself, he was not satisfied with an officer's life. The biggest reason for this dissatisfaction was that he thought, despite being an officer, he was just a toy to run the business of the British. Even with his wishes and willingness, he could not do vital work for the people of his nation. He wanted his people to have access to modern education of the highest quality, in order to fulfil the needs of their community, solve problems and contribute to the country's upliftment. He felt that despite being an officer, he could not do all that he wanted to do for his people in the truest sense. When Jagadish expressed his desire to take guidance for the Indian Civil Service from him, he rejected this proposal outright. Jagadish himself was surprised by his father's decision. He had seen his father doing his work with great enthusiasm. He felt that his father was not only proud of being an officer but he was happy to do that work. When Bhagban Chandra Bose forbade Jagadish to appear in the Indian Civil Services Examination, Jagadish wanted to know the reason behind it. In response, Bhagban Chandra Bose replied, 'It is a million times better to be a servant of your own than to be a slave to others. Be your own master.' Jagadish did not understand the meaning of this statement at the time. Later, this sentence became the essence of Jagadish's life.

At that time, Jagadish Chandra Bose only understood that his father's words should be obeyed. Bhagban Chandra Bose wanted his son to become a scholar. He had seen the country's agriculture in poor condition and had seen young and old people dying of diseases. He thought that the country could not prosper until high-quality agriculture was done in the country and the country's own people studied science and found ways to cure the diseases that were spreading from village to village as epidemics. He got this feeling because he was watching the British very closely and felt that the British did not pay any special attention to medicine, science or agriculture in India. He expressed his desire for Jagadish to contribute to the upliftment of Indian agriculture by studying agricultural science, or that he should study medicine to pave the way for its salvation from the destruction caused by epidemics. Jagadish would have to go abroad for this and Mr Bose needed to take more loans to send Jagadish to England. But it was Bhagban Chandra Bose's wish only. It was not yet decided how and where Jagadish would do further studies.

Gradually, Jagadish's mind started getting ready for higher education in medical science. At that time, there were only a few medical schools in India, in which education was given with minimal resources. A medical school was started sometime back in Calcutta. The teaching of medicine in India was at an elementary level. To get a higher degree in medical studies, one had to go abroad. Jagadish's mind gradually started to go to England to study. London was a natural choice in England. Now, the biggest question was how to meet his expenses in London. The loans already taken by his father were huge and he was still on medical leave for two years. It was not yet certain when his health would improve and when he would return to work. While on medical leave, his father was getting a considerably reduced salary. It was neither possible for Jagadish to go abroad dependent on the reduced salary of his father, nor did Jagadish find it appropriate.

Another hindrance to going abroad was Jagadish's mother. She did not want Jagadish to be so far from her. Having lost her 10-year-old child a few years ago, she did not want to send her only boy so far out of sight. Apart from this, there used to be a lot of superstitions in India back then regarding crossing the sea. Many people thought crossing the sea was against the traditions of the Hindu religion. At that time, the means of transport to England used to be by way of ships, which took a few months to reach London from Calcutta. Jagadish's mother had heard stories of all the ships going from Calcutta to China and Cambodia getting trapped in the cyclones and sinking, which were also true. Thus, she was terrified to send her only son to an unknown place amidst unknown people.

Apart from this, Bhagban Chandra Bose's health was also deteriorating. Jagadish's mother felt that if something worse happened to Jagadish's father, who would take care of him and the family? And in extreme circumstances, if anything untoward happens to the father, there must be a man at home. At that time in India, only men could perform the religious rituals in the patriarchal Indian society. It was impossible to imagine a family without men. Jagadish's mother used to tell him that he should stay in India and not travel so far. Neither Jagadish nor his father could avoid the mother's advice.

One day, a family meeting was held at home with all the family members present. A decision had to be made regarding Jagadish's studies. Despite his desire to send Jagadish abroad for studies, his father was forced to yield to his mother's arguments and feelings. Jagadish had made up his mind to go overseas by that time. But he also considered it appropriate to decide not to go abroad after knowing and understanding everyone's thoughts. He did not have the courage to go overseas and study and leave his family shattered. How could he be so self-centred when his father had risked his entire fortune and sacrificed his health for the sake of his people and society? Jagadish also agreed to do something in India itself. Still, his mind would wander here and there involuntarily. He could not understand what he would do by staying in India and what his future would be. This concern was visible on his face. Whatever the case, Jagadish's future had been decided in the family meeting.

Jagadish was sad and uninterested for a few days and tried to decide what he could do by being around the house. When he could not understand anything for a long time, he left everything to the future and started trying to divert his attention. Meanwhile, his mother got a chance to put aside her feelings and think about the boy's future. She could not bear to see the sad face of her son and felt that she was the reason for this. A sudden change occurred to his mother during those days. Whenever she would think about his future, she used to shudder. From her son's childhood, she had dreamt that her son should be more influential and successful than her husband—people should respect him. Perhaps this is what every mother would want in her heart, but the fear of being a mother sometimes overwhelms everything. Jagadish's mother, Bamsundari Devi, overcame her fear.

One day, she called a family meeting and gave her decision that she now wants Jagadish to go to London for his studies and fight to make his dreams come true. Jagadish and his father were surprised to hear this. After receiving his mother's consent, the biggest question still was about the expenses to be incurred in going abroad. Where would so much money come from in these times of hardship? With incredible difficulty, his father had already taken a loan from his friends for the tea plantation, whose interest was also being paid. However, the consent of his mother came with a pleasant feeling. Although it was very difficult for him, his father started thinking of arranging money. Jagadish's mother's consent did not have much effect on Jagadish, as he knew that the financial condition of his home did not allow him to be sent abroad and he did not want to behave like a selfish person. Hence, there was still sadness in his mind.

One evening, Jagadish's mother called him. Jagadish was feeling some relief in the shadow of his mother. Both mother and son were silent for a long time. Jagadish felt that it would be a very small thing to give up any dream for the sake of his mother's love. After some time, his mother said that she had arranged money for Jagadish to go to Europe. Jagadish's eyes suddenly opened wide and silence was broken like someone had thrown a small pebble into the still lake. Looking at the mother, Jagadish said, 'How is it possible?' Jagadish's happiness knew no bounds but he wanted to know how she could suddenly arrange so much money. His mother patted him on the shoulder and said that there was nothing to worry about, the loan had not been taken. Jagadish's curiosity increased after hearing it. Once, he thought that his mother was joking to ease his heart, but she could not joke like this.

Upon Jagadish's insistence, his mother told him where the money had been arranged from, but she put a condition before telling him. The condition was that Jagadish would not change his decision to go abroad after listening to his mother's answer. A little hesitant, Jagadish accepted the his mother's condition. Something seemed amiss to him. He wanted everything to be clear in front of him. His mother said that she had a lot of jewellery gifted to her from time to time, but she didn't wear much jewellery. The best use of those ornaments would be that Jagadish could study well. After talking to her father, his mother said that she had convinced him to sell the jewellery.

Many times, the dreams we have seen for years are about to come true, but we do not feel their happiness. The mind feels a bit heavy. Sometimes the sacrifices made by our loved ones for those dreams are such that they do not even give us space for a smile. The same was happening to Jagadish. He saw his dream come true. In front of him was the bright future that he had imagined, but the cost was not acceptable to him. Even if he had to accept this price, he was probably as sad about it as he was sorry for not being able to go to London to study.

His mother said, 'Son! I understand that going to Europe is important to you, and you need to educate yourself well. Because of your desire, I have made up my mind that every effort should be made for your further studies. As for the jewellery, it can be repurchased. My son's future cannot be changed again later. That's why you should go to London. I will take care of the rest of the house and everything will be fine if your father's health gets better soon.' She was trying to say that now she has removed the fear from her mind and will manage everything with his father. His son should return to his studies with ease and then take good care of him in old age. After much persuasion by the mother,

Jagadish agreed to her advice and after talking to his father, he started thinking about the process of going to London.

After this support and cooperation from his mother, everything was positive from his father's side. He was just in strict opposition to taking the Indian Civil Service training. Both Jagadish and his father now wanted Jagadish to try to change the condition of medicine in the country by getting a higher education in it. His father felt that Jagadish would be more independent and capable as a scientist in the direction of the upliftment of the country's people, than a collector. After a positive change in the family, his father's health improved surprisingly and he returned to his job in no time after ending his medical leave. This time, he took charge of Pabna, where he remained till his retirement. After his father returned to the job, his salary had increased considerably and now Jagadish's mother did not need to sell her jewellery to study abroad. Once again, everything seemed to be going well. Despite his father's high status, the atmosphere of happiness in Jagadish's family finally came after a long time.

Jagadish had decided to go to England. His father had come back to work from medical leave. There was a new energy in his father—he was watching his child and his dreams were coming true. Years had passed since he started his social life. During his lifetime, he had spent more time in the highest positions of British rule than any Indian could. Even after holding these high positions, Bhagban Chandra Bose often felt that he could not contribute to the prosperity of the people of his area, or pargana, in the best way he wanted to. He understood that the British intended to develop only that much in India that was needed for the British governments to continue to run properly. Knowing that the British would not try to develop more than a limit here, he himself often tried to think about and implement such schemes among the farmers and the youth in his area, about which the British were not very serious. He was primarily engaged in youth employment, a sound health system to fight infectious diseases, good education and being technologically prosperous to meet the country's needs. However, getting the most significant positions in the government department was possible only through the Indian Civil Service in the British government. In the British government, collectors or their senior officers would get many facilities and these officers also used to have a very high status. The children of these officers studied with the British and their wives would attend parties with them. All the collectors used to consider themselves British. Many used to treat Indians like slaves, sometimes just like the British. But in reality, if seen, they themselves were like puppets of the British. Bhagban Chandra Bose knew that he was a tiny part of the English machinery. He could only think about the welfare of the people of his area as much as the British government allowed him to think. Bhagban Chandra Bose got to learn a lot about the relationship between the British and Indians during the time when the epidemic spread in the area of Katwa.

He did not want his son to go into the civil service like him and become a slave to the British, even if he could sway and rule over other Indians. He dreamt his son would do such work that, despite being ordinary, he could either rise above the boundaries of the district paragana or do something for the good of the people of the country. Although this path was not easy, he made every effort to make his son courageous. From childhood, he tried to shape Jagadish in such a way that he should have all the qualities of a strong human being in whichever groove he be cast into. He should be courageous and responsible, but he should also be knowledgeable. In this way, he never stopped Jagadish from playing exciting games or doing exciting tasks. When Jagadish used to be timid in childhood, he hired a reformed dacoit to take care of Jagadish, who strengthened him.

After school, Jagadish's daily routine was full of adventurous activities. Nature was a significant part of his life, with all the plants in his small garden and the many birds, pets, etc., he kept in his home. He had been fond of horse-riding since he was a child, which was still intact. Jagadish also had a special horse that only he could ride. When he went to Calcutta to study, this horse used to be tied unnecessarily in the stables. It was exasperating for someone else to ride this horse by himself. Even Jagadish's father tried to ride this horse many times but failed. It was a very stubborn and obstinate horse, which knew its rider very well. When Jagadish came back home, it was as if this horse had come back to life—he would wag his tail with joy, as if he had been useless without Jagadish for so many days and now his friend had returned. Then Jagadish would caress his mane and from the very next day, his horse-riding would resume. As long as Jagadish stayed at home, this horse was happy and as soon as he left, he was like a dead animal.

There is a said story behind the closeness between Jagadish and this horse. When Jagadish was about 15 years old, he became more engaged in thrilling games and activities. This is another hallmark of youth, in which there is an innate desire to have more and more adventures. Jagadish had gone out for horse-riding on this horse and was roaming in a nearby forest. While roaming around, he went far ahead. When he was coming back from another unknown route, he found a canal on the way. The canal was in full spate at that time due to heavy rains and Jagadish had no idea of the depth of this canal. Although the canal was very small, it was dangerous during floods. Seeing the canal was small, Jagadish pulled the horse's reins, ordering the horse to cross the canal. Jagadish believed that the canal's depth would not be much but his guess was wrong. The horse moved forward into the river until it slipped in the middle. Jagadish was sitting on the horse's back and he too fell from the horse due to loss of balance.

After this, Jagadish, showing courage, somehow saved both their lives by swimming himself and helping the horse. Because of Jagadish's good swimming, he helped the horse reach the shore. After this, when Jagadish went to Calcutta for his studies, many people, even Jagadish's father, tried to ride the horse, but the horse would not allow it. Then, it became Jagadish's horse. The horse was sad and lifeless at home as long as Jagadish was gone. As soon as Jagadish came back, it would come to life and both would go towards the fields.

In his childhood, Jagadish used to be attracted to guns and shooting. He learned to shoot when he was about 15 years old, before starting his studies in Calcutta. At this time, a Rajput soldier became Jagadish's guru, to whom his father had entrusted the task of teaching Jagadish how to shoot. Jagadish soon became proficient at shooting with a gun. While on college leave, Jagadish went hunting in the forests of the Terai region of Bengal for a month. This hunt was a very new and exciting experience for him.

Now, Jagadish had decided to go abroad and study. A friend of Bhagban Chandra Bose invited him and Jagadish to go hunting about six months after graduating from college and before moving to London. In this time of happiness, Jagadish also desired to shoot and go hunting with his father. Then, something happened. Due to the busyness of his father, Jagadish Chandra Bose went hunting alone with his father's friend. This friend who had extended the invitation was a zamindar from Assam. Although Jagadish now had a lot of experience in the art of hunting, he was still a boy. The father's friend was a well-versed hunter, and Jagadish was still a too young. Apart from this, where they had to go hunting, big buffaloes, rhinos and other dangerous animals were in that forest.

Still, Jagadish's father allowed him to go hunting. He had no doubts about his son's shooting skills, horse-riding and bravery. Apart from this, Jagadish had to go abroad for further studies where hunting was impossible, so he was very excited about this hunt. There was also another reason to be thrilled that they were going hunting with such a big and famous hunter for the first time in their lives. It was like giving himself a gift before going abroad. Jagadish immediately got ready to go hunting, started making his hunting plans and gathered the necessary equipment. Since his father's friend was in Assam, far away from his house, Jagadish couldn't take his horse for hunting.

First, he had to travel by train. After that, his father's zamindar friend would pick him up from the railway station. The zamindar's house was 21 kilometres away from the railway station and a wagon was waiting for Jagadish at the nearest railway station before his train arrived at the platform. After a night's rest, they went out to hunt in the forest. The wagon itself had left them at the forest hideout. Throughout the day, they hunted on the backs of horses. His father's friend was an accomplished horseman and hunter. Those people kept hunting in the forest all day long.

The first day was very tiring and full of violence. Jagadish's body was not ready for such intense activities. By evening, he developed a very high fever. When the fever did not subside till late in the night, it was decided that Jagadish should return home before the fever became dangerous. There were no proper and adequate means of medical treatment and Jagadish was the darling of his parents, so the zamindar did not want to take any risk. But to go home, a wagon was needed, which had gone back and was no longer available. Concerned, Jagadish asked the zamindar whether he had any horses that he could take to the railway station. The zamindar had a spare horse and that horse was very good—it was a racehorse. But the problem with this type of horse is that such horses are only for a particular horseman. They do not like or allow everybody to ride on them. The horse was stubborn and obstinate and had tried to severely harm a new horse rider the last time. After that, no one dared to ride him. Jagadish's fever was getting worse. Burning in fever, he decided to try it once. The father's friend was a little scared, but he was sure that the horse would not harm him in his presence, even if it showed a little stubbornness.

The horse was brought out of the stable. As Jagadish tried to get hold of the horse, it neighed loudly and stood on its hind legs. He tried to bite Jagadish's hand and crush him with his front legs. Then, in the blink of an eye, Jagadish sprang up and rode on his back. As soon as he got on the back of the animal, he pulled the reins without delay and the gallop of the horse was heard. All this happened so suddenly that there was no time to bid goodbyes somewhere in the middle. Neither the father's friend could advise him to return comfortably, nor could Jagadish say thanks to him while going. After the neigh of the horse, the gallop of its feet was heard and it gradually faded away. The zamindar friend was worried that there might be problems on the way, so he arranged for another horseman to be sent after Jagadish. Although, it took some time and by then Jagadish had gone too far.

A small river fell between the zamindar's house and the railway station. When Jagadish was coming in the wagon, he had not realized the existence of the river because he had fallen asleep in the wagon. There was a bridge over that small river which was broken in the middle. It must have been broken recently. Jagadish had seen from afar that people had made a bamboo paddle path right next to the fractured wide part of the bridge. Horses get stuck in such places very severely. This horse was violent and uncontrollable. Taking any risk with this horse was not free from danger. But Jagadish was now an older and experienced horseman. He also had the ability to make decisions and implement them in the blink of an eye, like a hunter. As soon as he went ahead, he immediately turned the horse's bridle towards the footpath made of that bamboo.

The horse initially hesitated a bit to go on the trail but feeling the confidence of the horseman, he could not stop himself and proceeded onwards. Besides, there was depth and water on both sides, the river was fast and the trail was narrow. The horse's hesitation was only logical. If there had been another horse rider, the horse would have rebelled. Three years ago, Jagadish's horse had also rebelled before entering the water. Due to Jagadish's long experience of horse-riding, he crossed the river. By now, they had travelled fourteen kilometres and the horse was getting tired to a great extent. So, the horse passed the remaining seven kilometres very calmly. Jagadish began to rest after tying the horse to a safe place at the railway station. While waiting for the train, a subordinate of the zamindar also reached the station. He was late in reaching because Jagadish had come very fast to drive the horse so that it would not revolt. After this, Jagadish set out on a long train journey to Calcutta. He had forgotten his fever in this riding session but as soon as he sat peacefully, the fever again set fire to his body, along with weakness. After reaching home, the treatment for the fever started properly, but the fever was not completely cured and it kept coming back.

In the midst of this, his preparations for going to England were in full swing. Jagadish had only a few days left to go to England and start his university studies. His mother's concern increased as the fever returned again and again. Her only son was going so far away from her. His mother used to give him her undivided attention and his father kept him up with courage, telling him that it was just a simple fever that would be cured soon.

In the meantime, the day came when Jagadish boarded a ship from Calcutta to England with his belongings. It used to take about a month to go to England by ship. Jagadish was mentally ready for this long and unknown journey but had become physically very weak. Had someone else been there, maybe he would have postponed his journey. His mother was very upset and worried. But where was Jagadish going to stop and why would his father stop him?

The ship's journey started from Calcutta.

The journey from Calcutta to England was not so easy. Despite all the efforts of the doctors, the fever was not completely cured. Jagadish had become very weak due to a prolonged illness. His mother was very worried. After losing a child, she was continuously worried about the last source of light in her house under any circumstances. She repeatedly urged her husband, Bhagban Chandra Bose, to talk to the ship's doctors in advance and inform them about Jagadish's condition so that he could be properly looked after on board. The long distance from Calcutta to England would take the ship about a month. Her mother's heart was getting torn from the inside due to her son's separation but she was also happy that her son was going to England to fulfil his dreams and make his name. The land of those people in whose empire the sun never sets, who have captured almost the whole world. Her mother's happiness and the sorrow of separation had taken away her sleep and peace. Jagadish's father had assured her that all would be well and that soon her son would return to Calcutta as a doctor.

Jagadish was waiting for a new world ahead of him. He had heard many stories about England, told by his English classmates who were living in Calcutta with their parents. The road to the New World of the West was not a very short and easy one. Calcutta was left behind in no time and the earth's edge gradually disappeared from sight. Jagadish saw the expanse of the ocean. Although he had gone to the seashore many times, the vastness of the sea was visible only from one side from the shore. When a man standing on the shore looks at the expanse of the sea, he does not feel the same as the one who goes to the very middle of the sea and sees the vastness of it all around him. The ground beneath their feet gives a feeling of great security, which a man floating on a ship in the middle of the ocean cannot feel.

Jagadish used to sit on the ship's deck for hours, watching the vastness of the sea. Neither a bird nor any water creature could be seen far and wide. Only water and sky could be seen. The colour blue, which is a symbol of peace and seriousness, appeared to Jagadish to be himself. The sky turned ochre in the morning, red in the evening and blue throughout the day. Why did the sky change colour so much? Was the sky like those plants whose flowers bloom in the morning and wither in the evening? How did the sky know whether it is dawn or dusk? A young man immersed in thought, watching the sea from the deck of a ship, looked as serious as the sea.

Then, while travelling together, people would come and ask, 'What are you thinking, young man?' It was difficult for Jagadish to answer what he had been thinking. Jagadish saw a bleak future, as every young man feels typically at one point of time. The mind would shudder a bit thinking about all the things. The mind gets spoiled and then there is no desire to eat food or sleep. Jagadish's health was better than before, but he was not completely cured. One day, his body temperature went up again. It was evening. There was sadness in the sky which was filtering into Jagadish's mind. Jagadish, sitting on the deck, felt shivering in his bones.

He could not feel enough strength in his mind to even raise his eyelids and look at the sky or ask for help from someone nearby. He felt as if some fever was hovering over his head. What happened after this, Jagadish was told by his co-travellers later. Jagadish had trembled while sitting on the chair and started rolling down from the chair itself, then the people standing nearby had caught him with a jolt and taken him to the hospital. Jagadish had been shivering so hard and was in a state of semi-consciousness. As soon as he reached the hospital door, Jagadish felt as if he had been shattered. He slipped from the arms of the people and fell unconscious. He was later given medicine and transported to his sleeping berth on a stretcher. After this, the fever often kept clawing at him and on the ship floating in the sea, Jagadish kept wondering when he would reach England. The sea, which had initially seemed very serious, calm and mysterious, looked boring. At times, Jagadish got annoyed at seeing the vast ocean. Jagadish's body was getting shabby and the fever was not abating. To amuse his mind, he started reading Bengali books he had brought with him from Calcutta. When he was reading a book sitting on the deck, he heard two people behind him. They were talking about him. Someone was apprehensive and said, 'I don't know whether this boy, sitting on the deck and reading the book, will be able to see the land of England or not!' Jagadish felt very bad upon hearing this about himself. It is natural for a 19-year-old boy to feel sorry upon hearing of his death. For a moment, Jagadish also thought that the man's worries about his death might be true. That was when Jagadish realized that if he died in the sea, what would happen to his body? Will these people take his remains to England? Will his soul find rest without reaching London? Do these people even believe in the Spirit? Jagadish could not become friends with anyone on the ship. The questions were his true friends, in which Jagadish would often get lost. When someone sits down to think through questions, time slows down.

Amidst all the questions and uncertainties, Jagadish remembered his childhood friend and mentor, the dacoit, who had always taught him that a dacoit must be alert and struggling every moment of his life. The one point when he gives up is his last moment. He used to say that the life of a bandit is not very long, but he lives his life with full enthusiasm and excitement.

Jagadish was now about to reach England and there was more intensity and firmness in this desire than before. When the mind decides something, getting along with the body is not very difficult. It is said in the scriptures too that the body follows the mind.

One day, a piece of land was seen from the ship, which the ship's captain called the land of England. A wave of happiness ran across the faces of the passengers. People began to pack their belongings and were anxious to meet their families. Those who had left their families behind and come to England started collecting the letters written in their spare time and putting them in envelopes. People wanted to inform their families that their journey had ended safely as soon as they landed. Jagadish was also happy that his fever would be treated appropriately in England.

This ship from Calcutta reached the city of Southampton in England. Jagadish started his journey by train from Southampton to London. London is about 130 km away from Southampton. Jagadish was sitting alone on the train when he met two women and they talked a lot with him. These women were very generous and lively. His onward journey became very easy. The women in the train took great care of Jagadish. Apart from saying many good things to him, they gave a lot of information about England. Later, they presented some of their sketches to Jagadish while leaving. Jagadish did not forget this meeting even in his old age. He never met those women again, but he never failed to talk about them whenever there was mention of good meetings throughout his life. On his way from Southampton, Jagadish was weak, hopeless and in a rut. This meeting filled him with warmth and gave him a new hope. He realized that his visit to London would bring happiness to his life.

With this happy feeling and comfort, he stepped into London.

7

Brief Encounter with Medicine

London was a beautiful city. It was the capital of the British Empire, whose sun did not set in the whole world. As soon as he got off the train, Jagadish could see the glare of Grand London. There was a kind of simplicity in the air of Calcutta and there was an upper-class abomination in London. Jagadish had till now seen Calcutta, about which the great poet Ghalib of that time had said that the *khakanshini* (sitting in dust or modesty) of Calcutta was way better than ruling this city. And then he had also said that had he not been married and the responsibilities of the house were not on him, he would have left it all and settled in Calcutta.

London was the city of the rulers of the world. It is unknown whether Ghalib liked London, but Jagadish liked the city. An inquisitive person likes everything new. Jagadish wanted to know more about London, England and the mentality of the ruling half the world. What was it like in Britain? Jagadish's father was an officer whose masters were English. His father had status and money, but he was not happy. Jagadish wanted to know why his father did not allow him to become an officer after passing the civil service examination. Why did he want Jagadish to be his own master when it was a complicated thing and there was a lot of uncertainty in it?

The burden of debt on his home was due to the economic failures of his father. Even after this, what forced his father to wish that his son would become a doctor and save his people from the epidemics spreading in their society? Although Jagadish was educated only with British children, his father had many British friends and Calcutta was the residence of the British, he found that Anglicism was at its peak in London. Jagadish was now comfortable with the British. He had all his English friends who were good-natured. The British rule in Bengal was also going on almost properly. Even after this, what was it that made his father worry for his people and made him feel alienated from the British? Jagadish had seen the people of Bengal, but not much. He was neither very old nor had that much experience.

Jagadish enrolled at the University of London to study medicine. There used to be many world-famous doctors at the University of London. It was the year 1880. However, India's first medical college was opened in Calcutta in 1835 under the supervision of Lord William Bentinck, which later came to be known as Calcutta Medical College. But still, Calcutta did not have as many good doctors as the University of London and the facilities were incomparable. Jagadish had a BA from the University of Calcutta. For admission to the University of London, this diploma served as matriculation. Without delay and complications, Jagadish was allowed to get admission in the first year of medical education. In the first year, the study of physics and chemistry was almost the same as in Calcutta.

Jagadish was very comfortable in physics due to the teachings of Prof. Lafont at the University of Calcutta. He had no difficulty with chemistry either. Since mathematics and biology were studied separately at University of Calcutta, biology and plant science were new subjects for Jagadish. Although many modern

Indian universities have started teaching mathematics and biology in the same course, most universities do not teach these subjects together in the same degree course. In London, Jagadish was taught biology by Professor Ray Lankester. This was a completely new and exciting subject for Jagadish and his professor was a great expert and an excellent teacher. The plant science subject was also easy initially, so the preliminary scientific examination in this subject was easily passed. The actual study of medical education started in the autumn of 1880 and now subjects like anatomy and surgery had also been included in this study. Jagadish was happy with his studies and kept his father informed by writing letters.

Meanwhile, the attacks of fever kept on coming and going as before. The best doctors at the medical college were treating Jagadish and his condition was improving, but his fever was not completely cured. Jagadish's situation deteriorated as soon as he went to the dissection laboratory of the medical college. For a future doctor, what can be more frightening than the disease becoming the cause of disfigurement for him. Doctors found that one of the reasons for the frequent return of the fever was a bad smell in the surgical laboratory. Whenever Jagadish went to the laboratory, he would get a fever. Perhaps he was allergic to the surgical laboratory's smell. The doctors gave up when the fever did not go away, despite their best efforts. In this way, once the committee met, it was decided that Jagadish should leave medical studies.

Since the doctors were also the professors of the medical college, efforts were made to cure Jagadish and later it was also easy to decide that he should be advised to leave the medical course. Prof. Ringer, the well-known hospital doctor, also called Jagadish one day and advised him that he should leave medical studies. Life is above everything. Jagadish was disappointed after Dr Ringer said this. He did not have as much trust in other doctors as he had in Prof. Ringer. He had treated Jagadish for a long time. Prof.

Ringer was a great doctor, a kind-hearted and pleasant person who always spoke to his patients comfortingly. For Jagadish, treatment from this doctor was important.

Jagadish was feeling even worse than if he had been weak in some subject and had to leave his studies due to failing in the examination. He had to leave his studies for his health. His father had been ready to take a loan for this purpose—a purpose for which his mother was ready to sell her jewellery. After so many sacrifices, his parents had sent him to study in London. His parents must have cherished many dreams for Jagadish. Are all those dreams now shattered? Was the last wilderness of dreams shattered and destroyed? Do dreams also die prematurely?

When dreams die untimely, regrets and excuses, buried in the ashes of time, come to the door as an uninvited phoenix to read the mourning. Jagadish thought that had he never gone to Assam with his father's friend for hunting, neither would he have mosquito bites, nor would he have the fever, nor would such a big problem have come to the fore. Jagadish felt that dreams are like gunpowder. A wrong decision taken in simple curiosity can turn all in to ashes. Jagadish may have felt this way but was he responsible for this horrific failure? He was once again standing on a mountain of uncertainty, whose future seemed like a bottomless abyss. Should he go back to India? Will he be able to dare to return to India with such failure?

Standing in the face of uncertainty and failure, Jagadish thought about his dacoit friend and began to reconcile himself once again. Life and robbery felt so similar. He used to say that robbery is an evil way of living but it teaches us about life's most difficult situations. Looting is a brutal and reprehensible act that cannot be forgiven but robbers do not know how many times they have to make unsuccessful attempts. Somebody's hand gets damaged by the bullets in defence. Few have to lose their feet and few have lost their hands, but life goes on.

While living in London, Jagadish wrote a letter to his brother-in-law, Ananda Mohan Bose, explaining his position. Ananda Mohan Bose himself was an educated person. He had gotten admission to Cambridge University and had passed the degree of Mathematical Tripos with first-class honours. At the University of Cambridge, those who passed the degree of Mathematical Tripos with first-class honours were awarded the title of 'Wrangler'. He was the 'first Indian Wrangler' of Cambridge University. Ananda Mohan Bose advised Jagadish to study science at Cambridge University and he also wrote a letter of recommendation to Christ's College, Cambridge, in praise of Jagadish. In 1881, Jagadish also got a government fellowship to study science at Christ's College, Cambridge University, and he took admission there.

Once again, long-lasting fever had given a new way to Jagadish's life. Who thought fever would change the course of his life? Who knew that the fever due to which Jagadish had started feeling very low, would take him to new heights of success and fame? Life's trials are so absurd and confusing.

8

New Beginnings in Physics

It was the month of January in 1881 and Jagadish had a letter in his hands informing him about his fellowship to study at Christ's College, Cambridge. It was not so easy for Jagadish to study science there. He had to learn Latin due to its strong influence on science education in Europe. It was necessary to know Latin to study science in Cambridge and for this, the Latin language test had to be passed separately in the entrance examination. It is not always easy for an adult to learn a new language. Psychologists say that childhood is the best time to learn languages. To learn Latin, Jagadish had to store a whole new vocabulary in his mind. It was very difficult for a seasoned mind to cram new things. His stay in England helped him learn it. In January 1881, Jagadish passed the entrance examination and joined Christ's College to study natural science.

Cambridge's degree of Natural Science Tripos was considered unique because subjects like physics and biology were taught simultaneously. This degree was known for the breadth of its subjects. In the first year of the degree, the students had to choose two optional subjects from among the other subjects offered by

Tripos. Mathematics was an essential subject. History and the philosophy of science were also taught in this degree. After the second year, the student would get a BA from Cambridge.

Now, the last question was about Jagadish's life. Fever attacks were still recurring and Jagadish's health was not very good. The climate of London was not very suitable for a fever patient. After coming to Cambridge, Jagadish's health had improved, but the pace of improvement was languid. After some time, Jagadish decided to stop all the medicines for fever. For a long time, Jagadish was terribly bored of taking medications and getting injections. Stopping the drugs was a kind of rebellion which negatively affected Jagadish's health.

Jagadish stopped taking the medicines and started focusing on his health in general. He started going sailing. He would sweat profusely while sailing and swimming. In this manner, Jagadish tried to become strong internally. But of course, it was a very slow process. Once, in the middle of this, the fever took its grip so fast that even the college officers became worried for Jagadish's life. But nothing terrible happened. Jagadish had now decided with conviction that he had to fight this situation and face it firmly. Some battles go beyond victory and defeat after a time. Even if the fighter knows that he will lose, it is important to note how he fought. Jagadish also did not see any hope of coming out of this situation completely. But he was determined to be involved in this fight, while the best doctors did their part to take care of him.

Fever attacks kept coming and Jagadish continued to sweat while sailing. Jagadish's health slowly improved. In the beginning, the attacks of fever would come once a week. Then, they started coming every fifteen days, then every month and then there came a time when Jagadish found that his immunity to malaria and fever had increased so much that he never had a fever.

Jagadish was struggling in his life on both the education and health fronts and both of these were life-or-death struggles for him. In these struggles, sleep was alluding him for months. Various worries kept a black shadow on his mind for a long time. Not sleeping became a habit for him. After a long struggle, with all his efforts, his health improved but the habit, or problem, of not sleeping surrounded Jagadish. Even after a long, hard day of sailing, he could not sleep. Jagadish had to labour for six to seven years to get rid of this habit. In the future, whenever more work came in or Jagadish was worried, the problem of sleeplessness would come up again and again. Later, people inferred from the fever symptoms that Jagadish did not have a normal fever, but was plagued by the '*Kala-Azar*'. This fever had claimed the lives of countless people in the northern region of India. The cause of this fever is a parasitic bacterium still found in Assam, but its treatment has been discovered since then and now people have started coming up with ways to prevent it.

Jagadish's social life in college was also severely affected due to his ill health. Everyone wanted to stay away from him for fear of contagion. And Jagadish himself became lonely and shy. The first year at Cambridge was not very good for Jagadish. Although, in the very beginning, his teachers taught him very easily, the complexity increased later. At Christ's College, Jagadish found such professors whose names are still taken with respect and honour in science. It's not always easy working with the greatest of people or to live up to their expectations. It was not easy for Jagadish, but his inner zeal and enthusiasm were now supporting him in performing better in his studies. A new circle of friendship started when Jagadish began meeting people and his health almost recovered in the new academic session. The number of his friends began to increase. From classmates to seniors and juniors, they started sitting with him inside the college. They would go boating together and their friendship continued outside of college as well. Jagadish was a member of the Natural Science Club, so he became known there. In this club, people used to talk about all the academic issues, including exams and courses. The era of hostel dinners followed this and friendships at the universities were strengthened. Here, he met Mr Theodore Beck, who later came to India and became the principal of Aligarh College. Other friends included Fitzpatrick, who later became a physicist, Emmanuel, who continued to teach at the college and Reynold Greene, who became a plant scientist.

When he had started his studies at Cambridge, Jagadish was not very confident. He was not sure about his abilities. The name of Cambridge was known worldwide and the professors there were famous all over the world. Jagadish felt that it would not be easy to study here and pass with good marks. Despite his uncertainties and fears, Jagadish attended the maximum number of science lectures and decided to participate in the maximum number of laboratories. It was a tough decision and because of this, Jagadish had to work very hard. Taking care of his health was also a difficult task. But Jagadish was a stubborn boy and he was full of courage. Despite attending the maximum possible courses and labs, Jagadish did well in the examinations. The reason for this was the best professors at Cambridge. And who better than Professor Michael Foster to teach physiology to Jagadish? Professor Michael Foster had earned great respect among scientists at that time for his experiments. Professor Francis Balfour was to teach embryology and was among the most talented embryology experts of that time. Geology was taught by Professor Hughes and his wife, who were known for their affection and kindness towards their students. In this way, Jagadish studied different subjects in the first year itself and passed with good marks. Because of this, Jagadish's self-confidence grew stronger.

With the end of the examinations, the period of celebrating holidays started. For the first summer vacation, Jagadish and his friends went to the 'Isle of Wight' not far from London. Everything was going well and everyone was enjoying the island.

Jagadish felt like sailing alone and without any delay, set out to sea. But not everything was to remain blissful. His boat got stuck in a strong gust of wind in the Shanklin Bay and after three hours of hard struggle, his boat barely came ashore safely. The storm was so strong that it was not easy to save the boat from capsizing. A dangerous attack of fever returned once again due to this and fear. But because of Jagadish's vitality and the landlord's compassionate care, it was cured.

After the second half of the year, Jagadish started concentrating on physics, chemistry and botany. Professor Liveing taught chemistry. The spectroscopy lectures taught by him were fascinating. Although spectroscopy was not as developed as it is today, it was a great surprise to young minds that by observing and analysing the rays of light emitted by matter, information could be obtained about that substance. Professor Vines taught botany courses, and his classrooms and laboratories were highly admired. Francis Darwin gave lectures on the physiology of vegetables. Francis Darwin was the son of the famous scientist, Charles Darwin.

But Jagadish was most interested in physics. Jagadish's understanding of physics was better than other subjects due to Father Lafont at the University of Calcutta. Lord Rayleigh was the professor who taught physics to Jagadish at Christ's College. Lord Rayleigh had by now earned an honourable place in physics for his experiments and theories. His fame ranged from the Royal Society to the general public. Lord Rayleigh's teaching style was also fascinating, patient and knowledgeable. He taught classes with great ease, giving opportunities to the students to ask questions and solve questions with joy and enthusiasm. In the laboratory, he would train with a lot of patience and careful experimentation, which was reflected in his style of work. They try to have the maximum possible accuracy in the experiments and the minimum possible room for error. After analysing the results obtained from the experiments with a very high degree of intelligence, efforts would be made to interpret them accurately. Lord Rayleigh himself was giving Jagadish the training to become an excellent physicist—to become the shining star of physics. Learning the intricacies of experimentation from Lord Rayleigh after his introductory lectures in physics by Father and learning the brilliant methods of experimentation was like junior training followed by senior and higher-order training. Both Father Lafont and Lord Rayleigh must be complimented for Jagadish's journey in physics. While Lafont taught him the basics of physics, Lord Rayleigh taught him how to solve significant and detailed physics problems with maximum precision and minimum error. And, how to design a new experiment in such a way that it becomes a discovery rather than just an experiment.

These were the best days of Jagadish's life as a student. However, until now, Jagadish had not displayed anything that professors should note or even praise for the talent hidden in him. He was a very ordinary student. Jagadish may have been so mediocre in his studies that his professors were barely satisfied with his performance. Although people say that newborn's feet are visible in the cradle, there was no such thing in Jagadish's case.

Jagadish used to study and travel in England with friends on holidays. Every year he would go to different places—these ranged from wandering in the forest of Trossachs Park in Scotland to visiting the mountainous areas. The last year's long vacations were spent experimenting for a degree at Cambridge.

Jagadish received his BA in Natural Sciences from the University of Cambridge in 1884, and the University of London also awarded him a B.Sc. degree in the same year. For this, he did not have to do any work separately. Jagadish was not known to people when he got his degree from Cambridge but in later times, when Jagadish came to Calcutta and did his research, his work was praised all over the world. While leaving Cambridge, Lord

Rayleigh may not have been very impressed with him but later, Lord Rayleigh used to praise him very much. Not only Rayleigh, but also Professor Vine, Professor Darwin, etc. People praised Jagadish, organized his lectures in various societies and supported his visits to England. Jagadish had a good relationship with his professors throughout his life.

It was time to return to his homeland with two degrees from England. There was a sense of relief on Jagadish's face. Time heals all wounds. The struggle to save lives that had started three years ago in England was now completed and ready to give results. Jagadish now had to decide the direction of his future.

9

The Indian Dream

Having earned his degrees from the universities of Cambridge and London, it was time for Jagadish to go home. It had been decided long ago that he would return to Bengal and serve his people after completing his studies. Jagadish's morale was also at a peak at this time. There had been such love in the letters of his parents from home that Jagadish felt impatient to reach Bengal. It had been four long years since he had left his house. Jagadish was about 25 years old now and had become a mature man to render his services to his country.

After coming to India, Jagadish Chandra Bose received the news of the closure of the Bombay Mill started by his father. On 30 April 1883, he wrote in his diary:

> *Today, I learn that nothing could be got out of the Bombay Mill. So our all is gone. It leaves us in debt.*
>
> *Now, away from all dreams, I shall think of them no more. Let me wake up to sober facts. A crisis comes in man's life by the shock of adverse circumstances. Why should this not be the turning point in my life? Why should I not have the heroism of self-denial*

> *and learn to take pleasure in hard duties? I have all along admired independence, uprightness and indomitable pride under adversity in others. Can I not blend a little of those ideal aspirations in my ordinary life?*

He informed his brother-in-law, Ananda Mohan Bose, about his decision to go home. His brother-in-law was happy to receive Jagadish's letter and in response to it, he consoled Jagadish by telling him that he is known to many high-ranking officers in England and India, so he would talk to his friends for Jagadish. Ananda Mohan Bose himself was a well-known lawyer of Bengal and was counted among the people's leaders of that time. He was highly respected in Calcutta. Since he had also studied at the University of Cambridge and was the first Wrangler from India there, he was respected by his friends at Cambridge. Ananda Mohan Bose wrote a friendly letter to his old friend and the then Postmaster-General of England, Professor Henry Fawcett, urging him to find a suitable job for Jagadish.

Professor Fawcett was considered a very influential person in England back then. Professor Fawcett himself was also a Wrangler at the University of Cambridge. Today, he is considered one of the social reformers of Britain. At the behest of Ananda Mohan Bose, he told a friend and colleague, Lord Kimberley, about Jagadish and asked him to find a suitable job for him. Lord Kimberley was the then English Secretary of State for India. Professor Fawcett had asked Lord Kimberley to find a job for Jagadish in the Department of Education. But due to a lack of vacancies in the education department of India at that time, he advised Jagadish that he should go to India and find a suitable position.

After this, Professor Fawcett contacted the then Indian Governor-General, Lord Ripon, regarding Jagadish. Lord Ripon has a very important place in Indian history, but not many people know him in independent India. Lord Ripon came to

India in 1880 as the Viceroy. This liberal politician had made many revolutionary changes in the internal administrative rules of India. At that time, the indigenous journalism institutions of India were not allowed to analyse and publish all the issues related to the country independently. They could not condemn British rule in their newspapers. It was a crime to condemn British rule under the 'Vernacular Press Act'. In 1878, the then Viceroy, Lord Lytton, got this act passed.

Lord Ripon was a liberal politician and he believed in the freedom of the press. As soon as he came to India, he started making efforts to withdraw this act and, eventually, the Vernacular Press Act was withdrawn. Lord Ripon was a supporter of 'local self-government' and a resolution was passed in this regard in 1882 under his chairmanship. He became popular among Indians as 'Ripon, the Good' for these efforts.

In the year 1882 itself, Lord Ripon got the 'Hunter Commission' to formulate education reforms in India. This commission was formed under the chairmanship of William Wilson Hunter. William Hunter is the same person who wrote the 'Imperial Gazetteer of India' for the first time. He started this work in 1869. In the Hunter Commission, he decided that there is a need to pay special attention to primary and higher secondary education in India. Seeing the requirement for reforms in the Indian primary and higher secondary education, he advised the British government to pay more attention to it. The Hunter Commission also proposed paying special attention to women's education in India.

Apart from this, for the first time in India, the responsibility of primary and higher secondary education was proposed to be given to local boards and municipal boards. Hunter Commission is counted among the most significant works of Lord Ripon. Another bill was passed in the times of Lord Ripon, due to which Ripon had become infamous to the British and the Europeans. It was the 'Ilbert Bill' in 1884. Lord Ripon was against racist ideas and he wanted the feeling of discrimination to end in India. This bill was formulated in the name of Courtney Peregrine Ilbert who was a judicial advisor to the Council of India. This was one of the first concentrated efforts to end the distinction between black and white in the Indian Penal Code.

Before introducing this bill, the British had special rights in the judicial system. No Indian judge could prosecute or punish an Englishman at the district level. This privilege of the British ended with the arrival of the Ilbert Bill. There was great discontent among the British living in India and the people of Europe. Lord Ripon and the Ilbert Bill were vehemently opposed by the British all over India. Due to such opposition, the Ilbert Bill was re-passed after many amendments. Lord Ripon was not very happy with these new amendments. But even this could not demean and degrade his spirit to make the future of Indians better.

At the behest of Professor Fawcett, Jagadish met Lord Ripon in Shimla. Shimla was declared the capital of British-Indian rule for the summer of 1864. British officers used to stay in Shimla for the summer. The Viceroy Lord Ripon gave Jagadish a warm welcome and promised him that he would nominate Jagadish to the Indian Educational Services. However, in conversation, Lord Ripon told Jagadish that, in his mind, his life in India has been a failure. He came here to serve Indians and he had wanted to hand them over the responsibilities of their country. Everything seemed fine initially, but after the Ilbert Bill, everything went wrong. He had never thought that the British liberal traditions would be killed in this way.

After a good meeting, Jagadish came back to Bengal. Upon reaching Calcutta, he met the Director of the Public Instruction Department, who had already received a letter of recommendation from Lord Ripon regarding a permanent appointment for Jagadish. The director who was of English origin was not happy to read the letter of recommendation written in praise of Jagadish. He was furious from inside. As soon as he met Jagadish, he could not control himself and said with aplomb, 'I am usually approached from below not above. There is no higher-class appointment at present available in the Imperial Educational Service. I can only offer you a place in the Provincial Service, from which you may be promoted.' Jagadish neither liked this behaviour of the director nor his proposal. He immediately turned down this offer. After some time, when the Viceroy Lord Ripon noticed that Jagadish's appointment had not been included in the gazette, he sought an explanation from the Bengal government for the delay in his appointment. The director was infuriated at Lord Ripon's demand for this clarification. When Jagadish met the director regarding the reply to this letter, the director clearly told him that a lot of pressure is being put on him. He can give Jagadish an appointment in higher education, but it will not be permanent and Jagadish cannot claim later that his job should be made permanent. If Jagadish makes him happy through his actions, he will think of making his position a long-term one.

After this, the director gave orders for Jagadish's appointment to the Officiating Professor of Physics in the Presidency College, Calcutta. The matter does not end here. At that time, Indians were considered so conservative and rooted that there was a belief among scholars that Indians, caught in traditions and superstitions, could not hold the torch of science in their hands. Given such reasons, the Principal of Presidency College had vehemently opposed Jagadish's appointment. But the cancellation of the appointment was not possible due to the pressure from Lord Ripon. Eventually, Jagadish started working as a professor in Calcutta's Presidency College. He became the first Indian-origin professor in the Presidency College. However, his post was temporary and he had yet to prove himself to the British in

Science. This was a big challenge before him because the British had a particular prejudice towards Indians.

Sometimes mental conditions are so complex that it becomes difficult to differentiate between suspicion and prejudice. It was the same with both the Director of the Public Instruction Department and the Principal of the Presidency College. The most important point was that Jagadish had to prove his talent and this struggle was not as easy as it appeared.

Presidency College was an excellent educational institution in India. It was not easy for an Indian to get appointed as a professor there. If Jagadish wanted, he could have started a satisfactory job anywhere else. He could have thought that the British mentality towards Indians would never improve and that he was not obliged under a contract to enhance the image of Indians anyway. No one ever dreamed too highly for a young man who is usually ordinary in his studies. Jagadish probably did not even want to be the leader of the Indian rebellion against the British. What did encourage him to do all that he did in the next three years at Presidency College?

Jagadish had no hatred for the British, even though the most critical people in his life were British. Jagadish was attached to his people because his father was always concerned about India and had taught his child to love the people. Still, it was not so that Jagadish was now involved in the Indian freedom struggle. Rather, Jagadish considered this struggle as his own personal struggle. His father often taught him to 'be your own master' which is why he did not appear in the Civil Service Examination. How could he be his own boss while working as a professor in Presidency College? At that time, getting a place in the Indian Civil Service was an uphill task for ordinary people. One had to pass the Indian Civil Services Examination. He would then be entitled to every facility in the civil service that was available to an English officer equivalent to his position—equal pay and equal facilities.

But this was not possible in educational services. To get into the higher education services, having a degree from the prominent universities of India or England was not the only qualification required. Here, the nomination of a vital candidate was key. It was also important to note who was nominating the candidate. It was surprisingly rare for Indians to enter the higher education service. All the Indian professors in the higher education service were in the 'Local Education Service'. The local education service paid many times less than the Imperial education service and the chances of promotion in these services were negligible. Racism in higher education was so evident that until the beginning of the twentieth century, many Indian professors could not reach the rank of a full professor, despite performing very well compared to English professors. From civil service to courts, the British and Indians worked side by side everywhere, but this was not the case in higher education.

There was a wide gap between the browns and the whites. Where there was a dire need for both of them to work together to improve the country's condition, there was discrimination and animosity. Jagadish started making a place for himself there. In the next three years, he established himself as a responsible educationist. He worked to clarify the need for reform by giving his candid opinion on the elimination of racial discrimination in higher education and other vital issues related to it. Teaching in Presidency College was also not easy. There may be a distinction between white and black among professors, but there was no distinction among students. The students here were bold and academically independent. It would be appropriate to mention an incident here. Once, there was a dispute between two English professors and their students over some subject. And later, it escalated so much that the government was forced to form an inquiry committee that had no option but to appease both sides. Both sides were ordered to argue in discipline and within their limits. Teaching here was not easy for Jagadish, who came in as the new appointment. The students also would ask more complicated questions to Jagadish, assuming the new teacher knew nothing, and harassed him. So, Jagadish had to go to college with more preparation for his subject. Jagadish's other problems in college were more significant than this.

Apart from the local education service, there was also a lot of discrimination in the Imperial Education Service. Indian professors got only about two-thirds of the pay scale compared to the English professors. When Bose joined Presidency College, he came to know that since his appointment was ad-hoc, he was appointed in the place of some other professor and his pay scale was again reduced to half. This meant that Jagadish got only one-third of the pay scale compared to an average British professor. Jagadish had lived among the British for many years, but he was surprised to see this level of discrimination. When he protested to the college principal about this discrimination, the principal said that he could not have done anything better for Jagadish. He even felt that he should leave the job. There were several better jobs such as the Indian Civil Service, in which at least there is much less discrimination at such a level.

Jagadish also talked to his father about this. He suggested that the Presidency College job was respectable, where Jagadish can do something good for the youth of Bengal. If he felt that he was being discriminated against, he must oppose it wisely. There is no easier option than to run away from situations. It was not that this discrimination was happening for the first time. For many years, many Indian professors had been facing such discrimination, but no one had said anything till now, or even if they had protested a little, it had been severely suppressed.

After much deliberation, Jagadish decided that he would not accept this discrimination. It was necessary to oppose, but he was not sure about the medium of protest. What should be the route of protest among educated people in a top-notch academic institution?

Opposing injustice was essential and necessary, but how should he protest? With the change of understanding and rationality, the tone of protest changes and so does the path of revolution. Jagadish could not shift this discrimination by going out of this system. To change the system by removing this discrimination, he needed to remain in the job. When a small part that is installed in a big machine revolts against the machine, it is most likely that the part would break and disintegrate. The machine will be rerun by replacing it with a new part. It rarely stops working due to a small part's rebellion. The small part has to be very strong and vital for this to happen. So is the relationship between the system and the rebels. Jagadish did not want to break himself apart. No rebel wants that. There is hope in the mind of every rebel that one day the system will kneel before him. Jagadish knew the British well. They do not bow down quickly, but they also know how to bow before the honourable. So, the best way out for Jagadish was to strengthen himself first in the Presidency College. Jagadish's identity was very highly regarded among the British officers, but Jagadish was thinking of another way.

After much deliberation, Jagadish decided that he would do all the work given in the college with utmost devotion and with all his ability and integrity. He would prove that the Indian professors are no less than the British in any way. Apart from this, as a protest, he decided never to accept discriminatory cheques of less money that came in the form of the job's salary. He taught his students with all his heart and completed all the work of the college with enthusiasm but never accepted the pay-cheques. Gradually, Jagadish started becoming famous among the students. He used to teach the students after preparing hard to teach them well, listening to their problems and solving them. He was established as a professor who was polite, easy-going and caring for the students. He worked several times harder than the British. Many people asked him to leave his stubborn nature and accept the salary. Many people praised his work and said that he should get the salary, accept it as much as it is now, later these British will promote him. But Jagadish worked hard in Presidency College without a salary. It had been almost a year for Jagadish. By now, even the principal was aware of this, but he didn't care.

Meanwhile, more problems arose in Jagadish's family. Jagadish's father had invested his own money in many of his projects. He started many new ventures for the upliftment of his people, many of which were unsuccessful. At times, he had also taken huge loans. He had a passion for serving the people of his country. To provide education and training to the youth that could make them employable, he had opened small-scale industries to provide them with employment opportunities. For the health of the province's people, he had made many efforts at his level. He used to fulfil all these expenses from his pocket or take a loan. He also started a Khadi mill in Mumbai, which failed miserably. This mill was probably the first large scale Khadi factory in India.

Apart from this, he also started the People's Bank of India, which was very successful and later became the father of many cooperative societies. Jagadish Chandra Bose's father had struggled a lot in establishing this bank. Being its father, whenever the bank was in trouble, he had to buy many bank shares just to save the bank. When the bank started becoming successful, Jagadish's father started feeling relaxed. However, many of the other projects he had started failed miserably.

Meanwhile, his father gave many shares of the People's Bank to his poor friends and small portions to the needy. If his father had kept all the shares of the People's Bank with himself, many generations of the Bose family would not have lacked wealth. But the generosity and kindness of Jagadish's father was such that the family had to struggle for a long time and listen to the taunts of the creditors. In this way, his father's failure of industrial and agricultural projects fell on his head. It was a big deal to repay the enormous loans taken for these projects and the source of income was negligible. The lenders also kept quiet for a long time because they knew that Jagadish's father was doing all this for the public. With the passage of time, the lenders started asking Jagadish's father for the money he had borrowed. It was a time of crisis for the Bose family.

His rebellion and the economic crisis hovering over his home was simultaneously snatching Jagadish's sleep. There were taunts and advice on it from all the people who kept harassing both Jagadish and his father. People were calling Jagadish irresponsible and rude. They said that when Jagadish was supposed to take care of his house and help his father, he was showing his arrogance to the British, which was childish and unnecessary. It was not so easy to overthrow the British who were ruling half the world. Anyway, a long time had passed by now and the chances of the British bowing down seemed negligible. Jagadish was very hurt hearing all this. Problems from all fronts surrounded him. But he was strong and steadfast inside and he was not a man to run away from problems. This is also what his father taught him.

After some time, Jagadish started taking an interest in household matters. He sat beside his father, started helping him in various matters and started to understand him in detail. After calculating the debt, he calculated his ancestral property and later, on his father's advice, decided to sell it and pay off the debt. It was a time of great sadness and humiliation for Jagadish's family. Selling off ancestral property is a matter of embarrassment for anyone because the attachment of generations to the ancestral home is high. Preserving ancestral property is still a kind of upper-class tradition. But now, it was about to happen that the wealth accumulated by the ancestors in an upper-class family was going to be sold. All the relatives and friends of his father gave advice and warnings to Jagadish not to do it and called him irresponsible and stupid. He was even called a stigma for society and the family. The son, whose father had the zeal to run the lives of countless people at his level, was selling the ancestral land as his very first family decision. It was a humiliation for Jagadish too, but he stood by his decision. But the debt was so high that even after selling all the immovable ancestral property, only about half of the loan could be repaid.

Meanwhile, the behaviour of the professors and the principal in the college remained the same for Jagadish. But Jagadish had become famous among the students. He became the image of a responsible and high-ranking professor among the students of the entire Presidency College. It was somewhat comforting.

Jagadish took the help of his mother too. One night, during dinner, he asked his mother about her savings and assets. Every mother keeps ornaments and valuables for her children so that she can give it to them when they start a new life. Mothers also have small savings which often becomes financial help during bad times. Jagadish's mother was also keeping a lot of ornaments etc., for his marriage and other emergencies. Jagadish requested his mother to sell the ornaments to pay off the remaining debt. Initially, his mother did not like it at all. But later, she realized that she would be doing this to overcome her son's problems. So, she agreed to sell all the jewellery and personal property. His mother's jewellery and saved property were also sold off. But due to the enormous debt, only three-fourths of the loan was repaid. There was still twenty-five percent of the debt left.

The lenders were moved by Jagadish's sacrifices and they expressed their desire to waive off the rest of the loan, but Jagadish was a sincere person. He wanted to pay back every penny. He promised to repay the remainder of the loan to the borrowers in instalments.

Jagadish was about to complete almost three years working in Presidency College. Jagadish had not accepted a single penny from the college after working hard day and night, teaching and fulfilling other college responsibilities. The financial condition of the house had become helpless. Many senior professors and officers praised Jagadish, but no one took cognizance of his pay scale.

Jagadish's teaching style was scientific and straightforward. His classes would be packed and there would be no space to even stand in the classrooms. Gradually, the students of his class gave up studying supplementary made-easy books because Jagadish's teaching style was so easy and logical. He gave opportunities to students to ask questions. The same was true of his laboratory demonstrations. He taught them how to use it in an effortless and error-free manner. During the practical activities, the students competed for the front seat. When he became so popular that the principal could not survive in a position to suppress this matter, the director of the Public Instruction Department also got acquainted with all these issues and could not remain unimpressed by Jagadish's talent and hard work. He automatically agreed to give a permanent appointment to him with a full pay scale. Jagadish did not have to make any separate efforts for this.

In 1887, Sir Alfred Croft, Director of the Public Instruction Department, and C.H. Towny, Principal of Presidency College, called Jagadish Chandra Bose. They talked to him and later changed their behaviour towards Jagadish and proposed friendship with him. Jagadish knew this attitude of the British; they respected those who stood up for themselves. Both the director and the principal knew that Jagadish was firm in his principles. In this way, Jagadish's appointment was not only made permanent by taking out a special order but it was also approved to give Jagadish a pay scale equal to that of a British professor. Jagadish was given the full pay scale for all three years. It was a significant victory for Jagadish and any Indian professor.

Although this was Jagadish's personal fight, the pride of all Indian professors was at stake in it. When he won, he became a great example. At the time of his triumph, Mahatma Gandhi was only 17 years old. There was disobedience as well as cooperation in his rebellion, although he was not fighting for freedom directly as Gandhi. People may have forgotten this rebellion of Jagadish, but such a successful rebellion against the British should have a better place in history. After this victory of Jagadish, the attitude of the British towards Indian professors changed completely.

Jagadish was not to be stopped by worldly struggles or distracted by failures or wins. He was well in touch with the discoveries happening around the world and thinking about science. On 5 March 1885, Bose wrote in his diary:

> *I've been thinking whether the vast solar energy that is wasted in the tropical regions, can in any way be utilized. Of course, trees consume the solar energy. But is there any way of directly utilizing the radiant energy of the sun?*
>
> *Taking advantage of the heating effects, there have been attempts to construct solar engine which is merely a heat engine. We may also get thermos-electric current by heating one of the junctions. But such thermos-electric barriers are practically of not much use. Great amount of energy is also lost by wasteful conduction. Now, I have been thinking whether this could not directly convert the energy of light in to that of electric current.*

At that time, even electrons were yet to be discovered.

10

Repaid Debts and Unimaginable Loss

In 1887, when his appointment in the Presidency College became permanent, Jagadish's parents began their efforts to marry him off. They wanted Jagadish to start a household life now and it was the best time to do so. There was a kind of peace in Jagadish's house now. Jagadish's family liked the daughter of Shri Durga Mohan Das, a famous social reformer from Bengal known for his efforts in widow-remarriage. Durga Mohan Das was also the leader of Brahmo Samaj. He was originally a resident of Dhaka and had come to Calcutta in 1870. In Calcutta, he started practising law in the high court. At that time, the condition of women in Bengal was not very good. Even in Brahmo Samaj, women were made to sit behind veils separately from men during worship. After this, when some youth like Durga Mohan Das started making their wives sit in the open with them during religious activities, many people felt terrible and protested against it. After some time, it became a routine.

When Englishwoman Annette Akroyd opened her first boarding school for girls in Bengal, Durga Mohan Das supported her efforts and helped her financially. The school later merged with the Bethune School. The daughters of Durga Mohan Das were among the first few batches of female students to pass out of this boarding school. Bengali social reformers like Shivnath Shastri, Shib Chandra Deb, Umesh Chandra Dutta and Ananda Mohan Bose were his friends. Ananda Mohan Bose himself practised in the Calcutta Court, so his identity was through advocacy. Ananda Mohan Bose must have spoken about the daughter of Durga Mohan Das to Jagadish's family.

Born in Barisal near Dhaka, Abala Das had also come to Calcutta with her father. She did her early studies in Calcutta. She also attended the first boarding school in Calcutta which had been started by Annette Ackroyd. Even though her name was Abala, she was fast-paced and smart in her studies. She was one of the first female students of *Bang Mahila Vidyalaya*. She wanted to study medicine but she could not get admission to Calcutta Medical College. The reason was that she was a woman and the college did not admit women at that time. After this, in 1882, she went to Madras to study medicine on a fellowship from the Government of Bengal. At that time, women's education was not given much attention in Bengal. Going far away from home to Madras for the sake of her studies must have been a big event of that time. Her father's liberal and progressive views were a major reason for this. However, during her final year exams, she fell very ill and returned home to Calcutta as soon as the exams were over. She had passed her exam, but she never got to know about her result. She started working as a social worker in Calcutta itself, which did not need any degree.

In 1887, she and Jagadish Chandra Bose tied the knot. Their relationship was complementary to both. The behaviour and thinking of both were very similar to each other. Like Jagadish Chandra Bose, her family was also very progressive and respected. Chitta Ranjan Das, the famous social reformer and lawyer of Bengal, was the cousin of Abala Bose. There were many similarities between the two families. The marriage of Jagadish and Abala was completed according to the customs of the Brahmo Samaj. There was a wave of happiness in both the families.

Abala Bose supported Jagadish's struggles shoulder to shoulder and even after Jagadish, she continued his legacy and did much social reform work. Later on, she also established herself as a well-known social reformer of Bengal.

Whatever lump-sum amount Jagadish had received after getting three years' pay scale together, he used it to pay off his father's debt. But the debts were so large that it took Jagadish a total of nine years to pay it off from his salary. For six years after being permanently appointed to Presidency College, he continued to pay a part of his salary to the creditors. In this way, by 1893, all the debts were paid off. It was a comforting feeling for Jagadish and his family.

A tremendous burden had come off Jagadish's father's head. At the same time, Jagadish found the comfort of fulfilling his social and family responsibilities. For the last several years, he was mentally entangled in his family's responsibilities. Now there was no debt on him.

Bhagban Chandra Bose was proud of his son. The son was equally proud of his father. The pride and trust in each other gave the family the courage to make this big sacrifice. When Jagadish turned down the low salary, the house ran on his father's money. At that time, Jagadish's father gave a lot of courage to him. He shared his own experiences with the British with Jagadish. That helped Jagadish understand the British in India. And the most significant help is to provide mental strength in one's struggle. His father had been the backbone of Jagadish's life, due to which Jagadish was able to stand upright. He had been learning how to live life while watching his father. He had seen his father in good times and bad and how strongly he stood up for his people and his principles. His father's most outstanding quality was that he trusted people. This trust was probably because of his experiences or his quality. Few people have the confidence to bring a dangerous dacoit into their home and put him to take care of their child. Here, there was not only trust but also a vision. Even though Jagadish did not perform surprisingly well in his studies, his father always motivated Jagadish to do better and keep faith. He often told Jagadish that one has to trust himself four times before trusting others. Now Jagadish's family was happy and they were making plans for the family's future.

Not everything in life goes exactly as we plan. Jagadish's father passed away a year after the debt was paid off. It was an unimaginable loss for Jagadish. His father was like a banyan tree to him. Jagadish was entirely broken with grief. Perhaps now that his debts were paid off, he could leave without any remorse. By now, he had seen his son stand on his own feet. He was fully capable of fulfilling his social and family responsibilities. Among older people, this was a great satisfaction. Most people do not have any last wish afterwards. People like Bhagban Chandra Bose will undoubtedly have a last wish beyond this. Bhagban Chandra Bose made a lot of efforts from an early age to improve the standard of living of the people of Bengal. Some of them were successful but maximum attempts were unsuccessful. But sometimes, the importance of efforts goes beyond success and failure. His vision was inclusive, under whose guidance everyone could flourish. Now, Jagadish was left with his mother and the memories of his father and the principles he had been taught by him.

After his father's death, his mother felt very lonely. An unmistakable sadness began to take hold of her. His mother too passed away within a year of father's demise. Jagadish was not ready to bear all this. There was now an infinite loneliness around Jagadish.

Jagadish's life was filled with emptiness after his mother's death. Now, apart from Jagadish, his wife Abala Bose was there in the house. Even after six years of marriage, they did not have a child. Jagadish's mother had left for the heavens only with the unfulfilled desire to see her grandchildren. Their home seemed to haunt the couple. Jagadish started going to other places with his wife, Abala Bose. Whenever he got a break from his college, he would travel to different places. Apart from being with the students in college, this was now his primary way to relax. Jagadish's father had also built a house in Darjeeling. Occasionally, Jagadish and Abala would visit there.

One day, while sitting on the banks of the Hugli River in Calcutta, Jagadish woke up to an old desire which would often come to his mind during his childhood. He remembered sitting on the banks of the Hugli in his youth. River Ganges is known as Hugli in Bengal. Jagadish always wondered in his childhood where this river came from? Where was this much water stored, or was it made somewhere? What does the origin of the river look like? All such questions used to create waves in Jagadish's mind. In 1894, he began to prepare himself for mountaineering in the coming summer. He started physical exercises and workouts. Apart from this, he also searched for guides and porters mountaineering in the area of Gangotri. Jagadish's old desire to see Gangotri, i.e. the origin of the Ganges, with his own eyes was now about to be fulfilled.

At the right time, Jagadish left Calcutta to see Gangotri. After a long journey, the mountaineering started and finally, he had a vision of Gangotri. It was not merely a pilgrimage for Jagadish; his scientific mind had also been keen to see Gangotri for a long time. A seeker also wants answers to all his questions. Jagadish wrote a travelogue after returning from his Gangotri Jatra. This was in 1894 and this memoir or travelogue or article, whatever you wish to call it, was written by Jagadish in his mother tongue, Bangla. Its English translation is presented here.

In search of the origin of Bhagirathi

Ganga flows from behind our residential house. Right from my childhood, I had built a strong bond with her. At one particular time of the year, the river would come into a rush and dry up at other times. I used to see her daily in both tide and wave conditions. The river was like something alive to me, which is constantly changing. In the evening, I sat by its side with all my heart. The waves used to break the banks and the water kept on humming sweet songs as it flowed. As the darkness descended from the sky and the noise of the world gradually subsided, I could hear many voices in the hum of the Ganges.

I used to often ask, 'Ganga, where do you come from?'

She answers, 'From the tresses of Mahadev.'

Then, I would remember the story of Bhagirath bringing down the Ganges to the earth.

I have read many explanations about how rivers are formed. But every time I sat on the banks of the Ganges in the quiet darkness of the evening, I would hear the same answer,

'I have come out of the tresses of Mahadev.'

Once, on the banks of the Ganges, I saw the funeral of a very dear one. In a stroke, the refuge of love that I had cherished since childhood flew away like smoke. The love that had nurtured me got lost in some unknown earth. Does he who leaves this earth once never come back? Does he get lost in immortality? Does life end with death? Where does one go after death?

Where is my lost sweetheart today?

'*At the feet of Mahadev.*'

I could hear very clearly in the hum of the river.

As the darkness descended, the river seemed to say, 'We go where we come from. After travelling a long distance out of the house, we go back home.'

Whenever I asked the question: 'Dear River, where do you come from?' I have always found the same old answer, '*From the tresses of Mahadev.*'

One day, I said to Ganga, 'Ganga! Our close relationship goes back many years! You are my best friend. You have been so deeply involved in my life. The truth is that you are a part of my existence. I do not know the source of your origin and I want to travel with you and see for myself where you come from!'

I had heard that the snow-capped peaks in the northwest of our country are the source of Jahnavi!

I started my journey through towns, cities, forests and hills and reached Kurmachal, which is also mentioned in our epics. After finding the source of the river Sarju, I reached Danavpur. Then, I crossed many hills and peaks and proceeded towards the north.

One day, completely exhausted by this endless journey, I sat down. I saw a range of mountains and forests around me. A huge peak, tearing through the sky and hiding everything behind it, was the link in front of me. My guide said, 'Your dreams will come true if you can climb this mountain. Look at the silver line below. This later becomes the Ganges and travels across your country, sometimes drowning the banks in its path. If you can climb this mountain, you will be able to see the source of the Ganges.'

My guide suddenly said, 'Look at that side.'

'Jai Nanda Devi! Jai Trishul!' He shouted.

As I climbed up the hill, the view in front of me that had been a little vague a bit back, seemed as if someone had lifted the veil. The blue sky was spread far and wide. Two snow-capped mountains stood in front with their heads held high. One seemed gentle and kind, like Mother Earth, in whose lap all life blossoms, while the other was extremely long and sharp as if holding a strong spear—tearing through the sky and the earth.

I could see both 'creation and destruction' side by side.

'Your climb further is very complicated. If you keep climbing for two more days, you will see a frozen river,' said my guide.

After two days of trekking through hills, forests, valleys and caves, I finally reached the valley of snow. The melodious hum of the river that I had always heard suddenly stopped as if it had obeyed a magic wand. The fluid flow of the river froze in an icy silence. In some places where the waves were frozen, it seemed as if someone had said to the jumping waves 'beware'. It seemed as if the great creator had used all the earth's gems to make this frozen ocean.

Huge mountains stood on both sides with their hands up and at the foothills, an infinite number of trees were offering their flowers as a gift to them. The melting water was falling like a wound from the glacier in the valley below. Nanda Devi and Trishul were now immersed in the mist and were not visible. If I could cross the veil of fog, the hills would be visible again.

I travelled further along the banks of the frozen river. This river was coming down from Dhavalgiri. When it was diving down, big stones were broken and scattered far and wide. As I climbed higher from rock to rock, the air got thinner and the divine smell increased. It became difficult to breathe. Unable to overcome the exhaustion, I fell unconscious at the feet of Nanda Devi.

Suddenly, I could hear thousands of conch shells in my ears. I could see worship being held in the mountains and forests with my half-opened eyes. Water was falling from the massive stream of the holy vessel; the trees were offering their flowers and the sound of thousands of conch shells was reverberating in all directions. I could not even decide whether this sound was of thousands of conch shells or just the ice rocks thumping down.

I was thrilled and overwhelmed with joy when I looked ahead to see that the veil of fog covering Nanda Devi and Trishul had lifted and Nanda Devi's peak was surrounded by a sparkle that was hard to see. With the rise of the mist, smoke arose that covered the sky. Was it the so-called hairs of Mahadev? He had covered Nanda Devi like a roof. The snowdrops were shining like diamonds falling from the sky. It seemed to form a crown of diamonds around the peak of Nanda Devi, making the trident more pointed. 'Shiva and Rudra', the protector and destroyer; I realized the meaning of the legend. I saw with my own eyes how the drops of water, collecting (on the mountain) on their journey up to the sea, became steam and came back again. I saw the eternal cycle of creation and destruction with my own eyes.

The drops of water rip these bodies of giant mountains and break them. The rocks, thus displaced, roll down with the sound of thunder. The water droplets form a bed of ice at the bottom. As the broken rocks fall on the bed of ice, the drops of water say to each other – 'Come! Build a new world from the broken bones of these rocks.'

Millions and billions of drops of water collect their subtle forces and push these rocks down. In this way, the valleys are formed. Stones turn into dust due to endless friction.

Where I was sitting, I saw many big stones gathering. The snow melts and turns into running water, which takes away many large rocks to where towns and cities are settled. If a desert comes in the way, it floods and settles on the dusty desert made of worn stones. The desert becomes fertile from the bones that came with the water and in no time the green plains in the desert wake up. The flow of rain and water cleans the earth and throws the garbage with it into the sea and here another new world is created, which is not visible to humans.

The water droplets that flow into the sea are carried by the wind and from there to the coastal areas. After that, they flow inside the houses as if offering their sacrifice. The currents come out in the form of volcanoes tearing the surface of the planet. In the midst of all this, the earth trembles. The earth beneath the ocean bed sinks further to the bottom and in this process, many pieces of the earth come up from the bottom of the ocean and form new islands/continents.

The drops of water cannot rest even when they get mixed in the ocean. They rise again to the sky after getting heated by the sun. With the help of winds and storms, they again return to the mountains. Then, she goes there and rests for a while, until she is again lying on beds of ice before melting away. It is an infinite and endless cycle.

Even now, when I am sitting on the banks of the Bhagirathi and listening to the hum of the river, I hear her giving the same old answer to my old question, the question I have been asking for many years. But now I don't find it difficult to understand her answer.

'O river! Where do you come from?' Now I can hear her answer in a clear and loud voice:

'From the tresses of Mahadev.'

* * *

This travelogue is a testament to his unmatched writing ability. Even while reading this article, the presence of each and every element of nature can be felt very well. Such things can only be written by a person who is in love and Jagadish had an unprecedented love for nature. But since Jagadish was a scientist, he did not go out of the realm of logic even while falling in love. This love was not blind devotion. The result of the aesthetic sense came after knowing nature entirely with all the curiosity. But worth seeing is also the simplicity of this love. Jagadish's love of nature was so simple despite being a scientist. Few teachers can explain the 'life cycle of droplets' in such a simple language!

These journeys may give peace but after coming back from the trips, the complexities of life do not allow a person to remain calm for a long time. Jagadish came to Calcutta after a few days and engaged with his old life. Then, the same realities of life started hovering around him. Travels are unable to fill the loneliness forever.

People start by walking alone and empty-handed in the journey of life, but as age increases, the burden of life increases. Knowingly or unknowingly, this increasing load overburdens people with time. One day a man buried by this weight gives up on life. It is not easy to get rid of this burden of life. The weight of these attachments are so strange that man feels happy to live with them. He does not accept it as a burden. It becomes a reward which then becomes an integral part of life. Whenever all the bonds in a person's life are broken, he feels immense pain as if a part of the body has been cut off. No one calls life a journey just like that; life would have been compared to a journey only after going through the toughest of experiences. The same was happening with Jagadish. After the repayment of the loan, his parents died. All these years, Jagadish's life was dedicated to them. Along with this, he had to prove to the British in his college that he was capable and deserved the same respect as them. All these struggles were over. Now, there was a deep void in Jagadish's life. Attempts to fill the void in life through travel or writing were unsuccessful.

No matter how much a person becomes 'Buddha', he must have excuses to live life; even seeking 'peace' is also a kind of excuse for life. Nobody knows how much peace one gets by meditating in caves. But in ordinary life, whatever a person likes to do, after doing it properly, the amount of happiness and peace that a person gets is incomparable. What would be the condition of a person full of life, physically strong, but with all the excuses to live life taken away from him? Suicides are nothing but the process of sacrificing life by force and the compulsion of human beings unable to find excuses to live life.

Now, Jagadish was in dire need of finding new excuses to live his life. Those whom he loved the most in life were no longer with him. Jagadish would have filled his heart thinking that had he known his father would be free from life after paying all the debts, he would have left some debts to pay off later. Had his father been there, perhaps his mother would have also lived. A few years were spent in Jagadish's infinite loneliness and hesitation. Despite everything at the Presidency College, there was no possibility of doing anything new and neither were the resources present for it. Jagadish had no interest in active politics. In the process of thinking, he kept remembering his father's sentence, 'Better to be your own master than to be an officer and do someone else's slavery.' His father wanted his son to become a doctor and find a cure for the recurring epidemics in Bengal, so that people's lives could be made easier, but this never happened. Jagadish, at times, felt guilty and he wished he had lived up to his father's expectations.

His wife, Abala Bose, would often try to make him believe that Jagadish would make the best of his wisdom and that she would always stand by him firmly through life's struggles. It's a kind of comfort to be like this. After a long confusion, Jagadish decided that he would devote his further life searching for new knowledge. His life was now dedicated to solving the world's unexplained mysteries and simplifying human life. It was also a tribute to his father in a way' It was not that with this knowledge he would find a cure to the epidemics, but knowledge is knowledge. It will make life easy.

It was Jagadish's 36th birthday, 30 November 1894. Jagadish decided to dedicate his life to discover new knowledge. This would be now the purpose of the rest of his life. This decision was also a kind of rebellion from life and its circumstances. At that time, the Presidency College had neither proper laboratories nor other resources. Whatever handful of resources were available were in the hands of English professors. The main job of college professors was to teach. Jagadish himself used to teach so many classes throughout the day that he did not even have time to think about anything else. The load of teaching in the college was very high. The students especially liked Jagadish's teaching style, so he would have to teach more classes and students also kept coming after classes to meet him. There was no free time for Jagadish to think. He was not even trained in theoretical physics that he would sit anywhere and find new mathematical equations with pen and paper. The one with whom Jagadish worked in Cambridge worked in experimental physics. A laboratory and equipment was needed to conduct the experiment. And first of all, ideas were necessary for some planning.

Jagadish's mind was rebellious. He had heard stories in his childhood about trying to escape till the last minute, even after being surrounded by other bandits or police, and trusting himself. Every night is the last night for the bandits and every bullet fired is their last. Even after this, all the dacoits lived a long life. Every morning is the beginning of a new life for them. Stories heard in childhood leave a profound impact on human beings.

Now that Jagadish had made this decision, he had to find ways to implement this decision, no matter how dark the paths may be, even if there is a deep chasm ahead.

In the meantime, Jagadish Chandra Bose wrote the first science-fiction story which is considered as the first sci-fi story written in any Indian language. He wrote it in his mother tongue i.e. in Bengali.

The Runaway Cyclone

The scientific secret

First Part

A few years ago, a very mysterious event happened. There have been many discussions regarding this and articles have been written on this subject in many scientific journals of Europe and America. But till now, no conclusion has been reached.

On the date of 28 October, a news was published in the English newspaper of Calcutta through a telegram from Shimla-

Shimla, Meteorological Department, 29 September, very soon a storm is very likely in the Bay of Bengal.

This news was published in the newspaper of 29th – Meteorological Department Alipore.

Within two days, there will be a powerful storm and that's why the boats have been removed from Diamond Harbour.

The news that appeared in the newspaper on the 30th was even more frightening-

Within half an hour, the needle in the pressure gauge has gone down by 2 inches. Tomorrow at 10 o'clock, there will be a powerful storm in Calcutta and such a storm has not come in many years.

Calcutta residents could not sleep that night, thinking about what would happen tomorrow. Everyone started anticipating the storm with scared hearts.

Very thick clouds covered the sky on 1 October. A few drops of rain started dripping.

The sky was covered with clouds the whole day, but it suddenly cleared at 4 o'clock in the evening. There was no trace of the storm.

The next day the Meteorological Department sent this news in the newspaper-

The storm was about to hit Calcutta. It seems that this storm has moved in another direction after turning towards the coastal areas.

People were sent in every direction to know where the storm has gone, but no trace of it was found.

After that, the most important English newspaper wrote-

It was found that science is completely false / hoax in these many days.

Another newspaper wrote-

If this is so, then what is the use of keeping a useless office like the Meteorological Department by hurting the poor taxpayers?

Then, different newspapers said- *Close it.*

The government got into trouble. A few days ago, a temperature measuring device and air pressure measuring device worth lakhs of rupees were installed for the Meteorological Department. All that will not even sell for the price of a broken glass bottle and can the head of the meteorological department be appointed for some other work?

Being helpless, the government sent a letter to the Calcutta Medical College-

It is our desire that a new professor of plant science should be appointed here. He will teach about the 'relationship of human health with air pressure'.

The headmaster of the medical college sent his reply in writing–

It is good, due to reduced air pressure the arteries get swollen, blood circulation in these increases, it can worsen our health, there is no doubt about it. But the residents of Calcutta are currently under a lot of pressure due to other reasons-

1: Air	*15 pounds per square inch*
2: Malaria	*20 pounds per square inch*
3: Patented Drugs	*30 pounds per square inch*
4: University	*50 pounds per square inch*
5: Income tax	*80 pounds per square inch*
6: Municipal Taxes	*a ton pounds per square inch*

An increase of 1/2 inch of air pressure is like 'strapping a chain over a heavy load' Therefore, starting this new teaching in Calcutta does not seem to have many benefits.
But the atmospheric air pressure and many other pressures are relatively less in Shimla city. There, one can see the benefit of appointing the above professor.

After this, the government fell silent. The Meteorological Department survived this time.

But the problem about which there was confusion was not over. Once, a scientist had written in a foreign Nature journal that the rotating air has risen due to the attraction of an invisible comet.

These are all guesses. There are still many conflicts in the scientific world regarding this topic. In the meeting of the British

Association held in Oxford, a German professor had created astonishment in the scientific community by reading a very erudite article regarding 'The runaway cyclone.' At the beginning of the article, the professor said, 'The storm is just the rotation of the atmosphere. Let us first see how the atmosphere originated. When the earth was created, the air did not arise by breaking from a boiling metal sphere like the sun. How do these oxygen, carbon dioxide and hydrogen originate? It is a profound mystery of creation. The origin of nitrogen is also enigmatic. Let's assume that, in some way, the air originated. But the big problem in this is, why does the air not mix into the void of space? The root cause of this is the gravitational force of the Earth. Relative density defines the earth's force of attraction on any particular thing. Whichever has more density is bound in the same magnitude due to more force. Light objects have less force to them, so they are relatively free.'

For the same reason, if oil and water are mixed, then the oil of low-density floats on top. Hydrogen is a very light gas. Therefore, it is very much free and tries to rise above and escape, but it can't ignore the gravitational force. The scientific truth about relative density has been recorded that it is applicable in every place of the earth. We could doubt it, because of a country called India, where the male race being the owner of more power density is more liberated, whereas women with less power density are suppressed!

In any case, matter is bound to the earth's surface due to the force of gravity. Death of matter has a different story. When a man becomes a ghost after death, then there is no earthly duty on him. Some say that even after death, there is no salvation because even the spirits have to move about following the orders of the Theosophical Society. Matter faces death; it is a mistake to use the principle of death in relation to the matter. It is because radium gets divided into three parts and is transformed into the three ghosts of alpha, beta and gamma. Thus, the existence of matter disappears when matter merges into the void. But as long as terrestrial matter remains alive, it cannot leave earth for that time.

Although the professors used irrefutable scientific methods in this regard, why the matter does not escape from the earth did not say anything about the storm.

Only one person in the world knows the real reason for this incident (the escape of the storm) – that is me.

I will describe it in detail in the next chapter.

Chapter II

Last year I had a very high fever and I was in bed for almost a month.

The doctor said that I would have to travel by sea. Otherwise, there is no chance of survival if I get a fever again. I started to prepare to go to Lanka Island on the ship.

Due to the high fever for so long, the thick hair on my head had become rare. One day, my 8-year-old daughter came to me and asked, 'Baba, what is an island?' My daughter had just started studying Geography. She spoke before she could get my answer, pointing to a couple of tufts in the middle of my head as empty as the Pacific Ocean, saying, 'This is island.'

After that, she said, 'I have kept a vial of Kuntal Kesari in your suitcase. Use it every day on the ship, otherwise even the hair left will not survive (due to the salty winds) in the sea.' The invention of Kuntal Kesari is a thrilling event. An Englishman from abroad had come here to show the circus. The black-haired lion was the most surprising thing in that circus. Unfortunately, he had lost all the hair on his head when he was bitten by an insect while on board and in this country, there was not much difference between a hairless lion and a hairless dog. Being helpless, the circus owner went to a sanyasi saint and prayed again and again with folded hands, taking the dust

Sir J.C. Bose with his wife Mrs Abala Bose (1900)

At the Evening Discourse, Royal Institution, London, Sir J.C. Bose demonstrated his research on plants and the electrical signals produced by them. (May 1914)

Sir J.C. Bose during a lecture in Sorbonne, Paris (1926)

Los Angeles Examiner --- The Great

Plants Can Feel, Says Dr. Bose

'Suffer, Sleep and Get Excited'

Professor Jagadish Chunder Bose and his oscillating recorder with which he measures the pulsations of plants. This picture was posed specially for the Examiner, the first he has ever had taken for a newspaper.

The newspaper *Los Angeles Examiner* featured Sir J.C. Bose's research work on plants. It was his first photograph which was ever taken for any newspaper.

Sir J.C. Bose (1930)

India's first President Rajendra Prasad, who was also a former student of Sir J.C. Bose, paying his tributes to Sir J.C. Bose at the Convocation Hall of Delhi University during the Birth Centenary of Sir J.C. Bose. (November 1958)

During a technical demonstration session at Bose Institute grounds, Sir J.C. Bose is accompanied by Lady Abala Bose. (1928)

Apparatus for Microwaves generation and reception

Compound Lever Crescrograph

off his feet. The saints were enchanted and donated a dream-fulfilling oil as a boon. Later, that oil became famous worldwide by the name Kuntal Kesari. Due to the oil, the lion's lost hair regrew within a week. The power of this oil for a hairless man and his wife is limitless. For the good of the people, this good news was published in every newspaper of the country. Even the front page of the famous monthly magazine wrote about this wonderful invention.

On the 28th, I sailed through the sea on the ship. The first two days went well. On the morning of the third day, the sea took the form of a different idol once the wind stopped blowing. The seawater became transparent like glass.

I also got scared seeing the sad face of the captain. The captain said, 'It looks like a storm will come very soon. We are far from the shore–now it's God's will.'

After hearing this news, it is impossible to describe the commotion of fear on the ship.

Suddenly, the sky was covered with clouds. It soon became dark in all four directions and a gust of wind came from afar and started shaking the ship.

All of a sudden, I fell unconscious. I hardly knew what happened in between. Suddenly, the demons bound in chains got free and started destroying the earth.

With the roar of the wind, the ocean took the form of an idol of destruction by mixing the sounds of great thunder. After that, infinite waves came one after the other and started attacking the ship.

A high wave came over the ship and the mast and lifeboat were also broken.

Our final hour had come. As the memories of life awaken in bad times, I started remembering my loved ones. The surprising thing was that, at this point, I also remembered the joke my daughter had made about my rare hair.

'Baba, a bottle of Kuntal Kesari has been kept in your bag.'

Suddenly, I remembered one thing. I had recently read about the effect of oil on the waves in a scientific paper. I remembered that oil softens the fickle water.

I opened the bag with great pain and came to the ship's deck after opening the vial of oil. The ship was shaking heavily.

I came up and saw that a huge foam-like wave was coming to eat the ship.

I threw my Kuntal Kesari arrow aiming at the sea, 'Jiva Asha Parihari'. Opening the lid, I threw the vial into the sea—the oil immediately spread into the sea. In an instant, under the influence of Indrajal, the ocean took the form of an idol of peace. At the touch of the commensal oil, peace prevailed in the atmosphere. After a moment, the sun appeared.

In this way, I was freed from certain death, which is why that dreadful storm could not touch Calcutta. The many thousands and thousands of animals that were saved from untimely death due to this simple oil bottle—who will count them?

* * *

Actually, there is an interesting incident behind writing this sci-fi story. It was 1896 and Bengal was trying to cope with its manufacturing and industrial needs. There were several successful attempts in terms of establishments of manufacturing and industrialization. One such personality was Mr. Hemendra Mohan Bose, who was also the first Indian to manufacture gramophones. At that time, he had started a new brand of hair oil with the name of 'Kuntalin'. In 1896, Hemendra Mohan Bose started an award–'Kuntalin Puraskar'–to promote his hair oil product brand. This Kuntalin Puraskar was to be given to the best entry in a short-story competition. In this competition, everybody was entitled to participate but the only condition was that in the submitted story one should feature Kuntalin Hair Oil. In 1896, Jagadish Chandra Bose was the winner of this competition who submitted a short story entitled *Niruddesher Kahini*. It was basically a thriller story with sci-fi at its heart. Later, this story was included in his book *Abyakto*, (1921) a collection of articles and lectures, with the title *Palatak Toofan*. This sci-fi story is perhaps the first known literary usage of 'the butterfly effect'. The butterfly effect is an incident when a small initial change can result in occurrences of large-scale events later–like calming a wave out at sea takes the wind out of a cyclone later to make it disappear altogether. Even the term 'butterfly effect' was coined much later, after this story was written. This term was coined by Edward Lorenz, in the process of explaining Chaos Theory. Much later, Mr Ray Bradbury wrote his fiction 'A Sound of Thunder' which also included such scientific theory.

Jagadish Chandra Bose is popularly known as 'The Father of Bengali Science Fiction'.

Jagadish Chandra Bose was trying to find his peace of mind in writing. But he could not do so for long. Although he kept writing popular science in his own mother tongue, his mind was preparing for something greater.

11

Search for New Knowledge

Jagadish was now confused about how to begin the efforts to solve the innumerable mysteries of the earth. There was a world of incomprehensible riddles before him. The inquisitive mind looks at everything with curiosity and marvels. It is said that being amazed and making things magical is the first step towards scientific discovery. Jagadish used to marvel at nature since childhood. The question was, which puzzle should be solved first? The bigger question was which mystery is unsolvable and can be solved first. Jagadish wanted to start his career so that it is possible to mobilize resources that can yield results.

Raising resources for experiments was not easy. Jagadish did not have any support for his research at the college. There was neither any laboratory nor equipment. There were no partners nor any financial support for any experiments. Jagadish was now getting a full salary and all the loans were also repaid, so the only hope was to begin research by using the salary. With this salary, some goods could be bought and some small tools could be made. His wife, Abala Bose, reduced the expenses of the house.

The field of science is very broad and advanced and a direction was needed in this unfathomable ocean. There is a slight difference between science and magic. When it is understood how magic is being done, then magic is no longer magic—it becomes science. All scientists are nothing but the devil's children with the ability to turn magic into science, who, during a game of magic, try to sit in the front row to see the magician closest to him and understand the sleight of his hands. Their joy lies in being able to share the magicians' works with their friends and family after the spell is over and they can claim that if they have the magic tools, they can do the magic done by magicians at home. Jagadish also wanted to be one such child. He had the urge to see nature up close.

Now, he was in a quandary as to which was the first scientific problem that could be solved. At first, he needed extra time to think and read. After taking classes, he slowly started investing time for himself. He began to study various kinds of incomprehensible scientific problems. Ten years had passed since he had come back from Cambridge. In the meantime, the caravan of science had progressed a lot. In order to keep himself acquainted with the scientific progress around the world, he was constantly reading all the world-class journals and listening to the speeches of scientists from abroad. But he was aimless and without purpose. The work to be done was tough and needed to be planned well with focused efforts for a new beginning. After this, Jagadish called for the updated scientific journals and started studying them.

Although Jagadish had decided that he would continue searching for scientific knowledge, he was still looking for the subject on which he could do research. He was faced with the lack of resources and non-cooperation from colleagues on one hand, and the burden of teaching many classes on the other. In such a situation, starting research was an impossible task. But Jagadish Chandra Bose was determined to do the research work.

He turned over the pages of the world's most reputed journals to choose the right subject for himself. He read them and wondered if he could do it in Presidency College. He found some attractive subjects, but it was difficult to arrange enough resources in the Presidency College to research them, so it was impossible to research those subjects.

In this sequence of events, Jagadish once read a book by the famous scientist, Oliver Lodge, which focused on Hertzian waves, i.e., Hertz waves. Oliver Lodge was considered the great Maxwellian at the time. Maxwellian means one who believes in and researches the theories of James Clerk Maxwell. Maxwell first established a detailed theory about electromagnetic waves in 1864. His four formulas on electromagnetic waves had become famous at that time, but the experimental evidence of those four equation had not been made till then. The famous scientist Heinrich Hertz created ripples among scientists by generating and receiving electromagnetic waves based on Maxwell's four formulas. When Heinrich Hertz published papers based on his experiments, at the same time, Oliver Lodge had done the same level of research work on electromagnetic waves. On 1 January 1894, Hertz left this world. After this, Oliver Lodge, who had researched electromagnetic waves, became more important, publishing a very popular book on this subject. In 1894, this book was acquired by Jagadish Chandra Bose. From here, the direction of his detailed research was determined. Bose's student, N.C. Nag, mentioned that in 1892–1894, Bose had demonstrated the elementary experiments of Tesla and Hertz to the students in his classes by simplifying them. Still, all that was only to explain the subject to his students.

While reading Oliver Lodge's book, Jagadish Chandra Bose felt that this was the subject he should be working on. However, he had neither a laboratory nor any equipment. But seeing the equipment used by Hertz and Oliver in the book, he felt that such advanced equipment could be made in Calcutta. Yet it was necessary to be sure about it before starting work. An old friend and colleague of Jagadish Chandra Bose, Acharya P.C. Ray, was already doing chemistry research in Calcutta. Acharya P.C. Ray encouraged Bose a lot and boosted his morale.

Jagadish Chandra Bose did not have any free space to set up the laboratory, nor would the Principal of the Presidency College give him a new place. So, Jagadish converted his sitting chamber at Presidency College into a laboratory. Now, the subsequent requirement was designing the equipment for use. Jagadish took an unemployed blacksmith along with him and decided to make use of his equipment for his experiments. He also required money from which the necessary things would be bought and wages would be paid in return for the work. With no financial help from anywhere, Jagadish started using money from his salary. He had to reduce all the household expenses. Eventually, he created a tool with the help of a roadside carpenter and a blacksmith. Jagadish wanted to use this device to solve the most complex problem of physics of that time in the world. When his fellow British teachers came to know about this, they laughed in the streets and squares talking about Bose. Sometimes these laughs were so strong that their echoes would reach Jagadish's ears. But Jagadish was least concerned about the result. He just wanted to give his best.

Jagadish Chandra Bose began to work with tools made by the untrained blacksmiths and carpenters having their small shops near the college campus. He would be engrossed in his new equipment till late in the evening and sometimes till night after retiring from his classes. Being created by novices, there were many shortcomings in the device and its parts which Jagadish gradually understood and removed. After certain attempts, the equipment started working. The best thing was that Jagadish began to get good results from the beginning itself. By the end of the students' examinations, Jagadish had some significant results from this experiment. After the investigations, Professor Bose checked his results several times. It was also necessary because he was working on this subject for the first time and he did not have any particular experience related to this subject. Professor Bose was trying to decide whether there was any problem with the method and the equipment of his use. After many tests, when Jagadish was satisfied with the results of his experiments, he started writing his first research paper based on these results.

In May 1895, Bose sent the first paper to be published in the prestigious *Journal of Asiatic Society of Bengal*. The research paper was published in the 64th issue of this journal in the year 1896. Its title was 'On the Polarization of Electric Rays by Double Refractive Crystals'. This paper became very popular among contemporary scientists and Jagadish received huge applause. Jagadish published two more papers in the famous journal *The Electrician* in the year 1895 on the optical properties of these electric waves. The other research paper was on his equipment and its title was 'On a new Electropolariscope' in *The Electrician*. *The Electrician* was published in London and was the leading journal of telegraphy and electricity at that time. It was a matter of great pride to be published in this journal at that time. Further, publishing on the equipment designed was something very special till then.

In the meantime, Jagadish Chandra Bose was invited to the Town Hall of Calcutta to talk in detail about his research discoveries. At that time, it was a trend among scientists that they used to give speeches to inform the public about their research and the exciting results. This practice was prevalent in the West. In the West, people flocked to listen to the speeches of Sir Humphrey Devi and Sir Michael Faraday in the nineteenth century. The Town Hall of Calcutta was packed that day. Sir Alexander McKenzie, Lieutenant Governor of Bengal Residency, was present to listen to this speech from Jagadish Chandra Bose. Apart from him, many professors, scientists, students, intellectuals and the general public were present. Jagadish Chandra Bose had properly set all his equipment to perform the experiments much before the given time. When he was ready to perform the experiments, he thought about the main points of his speech and then waited for the given time. Slowly, the Town Hall of Calcutta filled up. Professor Bose started giving his talk and explaining these waves. He then went to the equipment to perform his experiments.

In 1895, Jagadish performed two experiments at the Town Hall of Calcutta. He set fire to gunpowder about 75 feet away without touching it and fired the pistol kept at such a distance without pressing its trigger. It was nothing less than magic for the general public. Professor Bose was now explaining that he did all this with the help of invisible electromagnetic waves. These electromagnetic waves (people used to call them electric waves at that time) were not visible, the waves covered long distances in a very short time and their speed was equal to the speed of light. And the special quality was that it used to cross through a person's body by penetrating it. The experiments demonstrated were examples of wireless communication. Jagadish was performing this demonstration in the Town Hall of Calcutta in 1895, almost contemporary to Alexander Stepanovich Popov's publication and almost two years before Marconi, who is called the father of 'wireless communication'. Demonstrating the technique to British government officials, Jagadish established himself in the field in an incredibly short time. Now, the discussions of his successes were happening all over the world.

People called Jagadish one of the pioneers of wireless communication. But the race to establish this new type of wireless communication involved scientists from all over the world. Marconi was later accepted as the father of wireless communication. Many people still consider Jagadish Chandra Bose as the father of wireless communication instead. But this story is not so straight and flat. The story of the development of wireless communication is exciting. This fight, or race, was not one-sided and the future of the development of electromagnetic waves was also associated with it.

12

Inventor of Wireless Communication: Papov, Bose or Marconi

The story of modern wireless communication technology and microwaves goes hand in hand. There are many ups and downs in this story. Wireless communication was not a new idea in the year 1895. Scientists worldwide had already made many discoveries in this direction, but they could not find what some people had dreamed. It was the only Holy Grail the scientists were after.

This story begins with information communication. Centuries before 1895, in 1400, a human being was born in Germany whose name was Johannes Gutenberg. Mr Gutenberg was responsible for making the world's first printing press due to which there was a revolution in moving information from one place to another. In fact, communication has a very close relationship with power. The printing press was used extensively in the sixteenth century by religious people along with the rebels to spread the rule of trade. Another great discovery that followed this in the nineteenth century was the telegraph. Through the telegraph, people would transfer their writing from one place to another and in this process, no one had to go to another person with the envelope in their hand. After some time, this distance increased. With the help of telegraph lines, messages were also sent from one country to another.

On 9 October 1874, a meeting of people associated with the International Postal Service was held at Bern, where it was decided that mail would not be confined to the borders of one country. It is called the 'Treaty of Bern'. However, it took many more years for telegraph messaging to become successful on a global scale. The International Telegraphy Union was formed on 17 May 1865. In telegraphy, wires were used to send messages from one place to another. This facility was limited to selected locations in the country. Sometimes, phone lines were also used to transmit telegraph messages. By 1895, telegraphy had become very popular, but it had many limitations.

Wireless telegraphy was probably first conceived in writing in 1795 by Francisco Salva Campillo of Spain. He originally wrote an article advising the use of electricity through wires in telegraphy. In the same article, he also said, very loosely, that a day would come when these conducting wires would not even be needed to send messages by telegraph. Salve was originally a physician and is remembered because he left behind a huge medical library in Barcelona.

In 1789, an assistant to the physician Luigi Galvani of Bologna, Italy, observed that a scalpel in the leg of an amputated frog produced a stir when there was a spark nearby. He told this to Luigi Galvani. Being a medical doctor, Galvani did not pay much attention to this. It is said that if Galvani had known about electromagnetism and had been a physicist, he would have invented wireless telegraphy at the same time. The basis for saying this is that when Marconi installed wireless telegraphy in Europe in the twentieth century, the French physiologist Lefevre mounted a spark transmitter on the Eiffel Tower and generated a spark. He had also connected a frog with a signal recorder at Raines, about 200 miles from the Eiffel Tower. After this, it was seen that the signal that was sent from the spark transmitter from the Eiffel Tower was recorded in the leg of the frog. But since Lefevre was not a physicist, he lost his golden opportunity to discover wireless signalling.

Another invention was made in 1837: the Electric Telegraph. It was not one but two people who invented it in different countries. It was the result of the ongoing discussions on electric machines. Electric machines were the new trend. It is another matter that it was too late for the invention of the electron then. The discoverer of the electron was not even born then. But people's attention towards electricity and magnetism had started to increase quite a lot. In the United States, William Cooke patented the electric telegraph and Charles Wheatstone did the same in the UK. It was also commercialized in England. It was used in 1839 along the newly built Great Western Railway from Paddington Station in London to the town of West Drayton. These two stations were 21 kilometres apart.

In 1837, Samuel Morse demonstrated an improved version of the electric telegraph at New York University, through which he sent messages a distance of about a quarter of a mile. By 1844, Samuel Morse had connected Washington DC and Baltimore by electric telegraph. There is a distance of about 64 kilometres between them. Another advantage of this telegraph was that the message was sent through a code written in binary mode, consisting of dots and dashes. This electric telegraph and its coding were very simple. Many consider it to be an early version of digital communication. It was followed by a flood of different versions of electric telegraphs. In 1849, Antonio Meucci demonstrated a telephone in Havana, the capital of Cuba. Although since he was not knowledgeable about the US patent system, he could not patent his design or take any advantage of his invention.

The world's first telephone was patented in the name of Alexander Graham Bell in 1876. An electromagnetic voice transmitter, i.e., the electromagnetic sound broadcaster, was installed in this telephone. The exciting point is that after exactly two hours, Elisha Gray also reached the patent office with a design similar to the design of Graham Bell. However, according to the US patent laws of 1876, the patent was granted to the one who invented the technology first, not the one who reached the office first. Although everyone knows that later the decision was made by the court in favour of Graham Bell, hardly anyone has heard the name of Elisha Gray. But the interesting point about this is that Alexander Graham got the patent to 'revise telegraphy'. It had emerged as the most talked-about patented case of that time. There were more than 600 applications against this patent candidacy, in which Graham Bell won. After this, Graham Bell opened the Bell Telephone Company in 1877. The International Bell Telephone Company was established in Brussels. By 1886, more than 1.5 million telephones were working in America. Although Morse's telegraph significantly increased the distance the signal could be transmitted, Graham Bell's telephone allowed voice to be used instead of a written message.

Around 1851, another machine, 'Snail Telegraph', was heard of. The then journalist and feminist, Jules Alix, had mentioned this strange machine Jacques Toussaint Benoit built. She said that she connected the whole of Paris with this, but that the technology was not for long-distance. Benoit suddenly disappeared after some time and after that, there was no news of him.

In the meantime, people kept adopting new and innovative ways to transmit sound from one place to another for short distances. There is a place in the Golconda Fort near Hyderabad in India where the sound automatically reaches about half a mile away. It is a fine example of acoustics and workmanship. After all his efforts, Mahlon Loomis, a dental specialist in America, filed a patent in 1850 regarding the wireless communication system, which he finally got in 1872. This design is said to be the world's first patent in wireless telecommunication. Through this, Loomis sent messages up to 21 kilometres away via the wireless system. He called it the 'Aerial Telegraph'. Loomis wrote in his patent application, 'It will be used to transmit and receive electric vibrations in the aerial environment.' These vibrations would travel from one place to another through the atmosphere and the earth. In 1869, the American Congress promised to give US $50,000 to Loomis for the assistance provided to make this machine. But later, Loomis could not develop any such technology. Although many people were working to develop a wireless communication system, one such person was David Edward Hughes in England, who made a device to amplify sound. Hughes called it the microphone and displayed it to the Royal Society on 8 May 1878. They did not patent it and the part was quickly incorporated into the bull's phone.

Apart from these, it is important to mention another scientist here: Nathan Stubblefield. He was from Kentucky, USA. People say that Stubblefield started working on acoustics in 1880 and designed a simple device like a wireless telephone. He also demonstrated his equipment to the people of Moore and communicated information without wires for a distance of about 250 feet. He also got a patent for this in 1907, but when people insisted on making equipment for it, he stopped working in this direction.

Apart from all these efforts in wireless information communication, some other efforts were being made in physics. Its beginning can be considered to be since Faraday proved the principle of unity in electricity and magnetism. Faraday proved that electricity and magnetism are two sides of the same coin. When Jacob Henry was trying to convert magnetism into electricity in America in 1831, Michael

Faraday in England tried to establish a relationship between electricity and magnetism.

In 1864, the famous scientist, James Clerk Maxwell, theoretically proved that light has electromagnetic waves using unitary formulas of electricity and magnetism. Thus, at the theoretical level, Maxwell proved that light is the only small window of electromagnetic waves that we can see. Depending on the frequency of these waves, there should also be invisible waves with properties like light, whose frequency will be either more or less than the frequency of light. But the problem was that since these waves were not visible to us, it was difficult for scientists to generate them, detect them and understand and analyze their properties. Thus, based on Maxwell's theoretical prediction, efforts to find these high- and low-frequency electromagnetic waves began.

This emerged as a big challenge for the scientists. We had eyes to see the light and many ways to generate it, but from generating these invisible waves to detecting them, scientists had to find new tools. There was fierce competition among the scientists in the laboratory. The names of two scientists should be mentioned prominently in this competition—Heinrich Hertz and Oliver Lodge. Even before Maxwell's death, Oliver Lodge was engaged in the discovery of electromagnetic waves at his University of Liverpool. Still, he did not yet know how to generate and detect these invisible waves. Heinrich Hertz took the lead in this race.

Heinrich Hertz was still a very young boy. Hertz's mentor at the University of Berlin was Hermann Helmholtz, a highly respected physics figure. He was the one who inspired Hertz to research electromagnetic waves. This was at the time of 1887. Hertz generated and detected these invisible waves of a certain frequency in Karlsruhe, Germany. The frequency of these waves was less than the frequency of light. In this way, Hertz was accepted as the first scientist to indisputably discover electromagnetic waves of a frequency lower than that of light. At the time, Hertz was only 27 years old. In his honour, the unit of 'cycles per second' associated with frequency came to be called 'hertz'. In 1888, Hertz published a paper related to these results. A long-time dream of Maxwellians came true after this discovery. Maxwellians respected Hertz very much. Heinrich Hertz died an untimely death in 1894 at the age of 36.

According to Maxwell's principle, there is a range of frequencies below and above the frequency of visible light. Hertz began by finding waves of only one frequency out of this wide range, but the real work was yet to be done. In particular, waves with frequencies lower than light could be used in all technical fields. High-frequency electromagnetic waves could be used in a variety of technical fields but creating and deploying them was difficult. After Hertz, Oliver Lodge emerged as the leading Maxwellian. Oliver Lodge did great work on low-frequency electromagnetic waves.

Apart from Hertz, Thomas Alva Edison also made efforts in this direction, but he could not properly understand these waves theoretically and failed to generate and detect them. In his patent application, Thomas Alva Edison wrote, 'I have discovered that if electric telegraphy signals are sent at a sufficient height above the earth to prevent the absorption of waves by the atmosphere and to overcome the curvature of the earth, these signals can be sent over long distances without the help of wires.' Edison had been trying to send signals from one place to another without the help of wires since 1870. However, when he was standing at the edge of the discovery of electromagnetic waves, he stopped making efforts in this direction and started solving other problems. In the meantime, Edison had also patented a device known as the 'Grasshopper Telegraph' but did not work on it further.

William H. Preece also falls into this category. He made all efforts to develop a wireless communication system in England but failed. Preece believed that the Maxwellian people were not interested in wireless communication at all. They only wanted to find microwaves, i.e., waves with a frequency lower than light, for their own scientific purposes only. This was true to an extent. Hertz also did not care about telegraphy or wireless communication. The idea that Hertz waves can be used in telecommunications was first put forth by England's leading physicist, William Crookes, in an essay in the magazine *Fortnightly Review* in 1892. About four years later, the name Marconi was heard in this area. However, Marconi denied reading Crooks' article before applying for his patent.

After Hertz's death, Ernst Rutherford also made efforts to advance his experiments by improving Hertz's instruments. Apart from this, Oliver Lodge had also made the most effective contribution in this direction. He had greatly improved the receiver made by Hertz. It was greatly improved by Lodge in England and Edward Brenley in France by making several changes to Hertz's receiver during different attempts. Lodge named this new receiver 'Coherer'.

Oliver Lodge was a direct rival of Marconi, so Marconi always took care of his own matters. When Lodge accused Marconi of stealing his receiver's design, Marconi always insisted he used the 'Brenley receiver' innovation in his patented design. Similarly, Marconi's neighbour, Augusto Righi, improved the transmitter as well. He called this new transmitter a 'spark oscillator'. Righi started this work in the year 1889. Marconi also admitted that he used a 'Righi Oscillator'. In 1896, Marconi came to England very hurriedly and applied for a patent. Although it is clear that Jagadish Chandra Bose did this work only in 1895, his transmitter and receiver designs were made by himself completely indigenously.

Another important name is Alexander Popov of Russia. Popov also demonstrated his device to the Russian Society of Physics and Chemistry on 7 May 1895. He demonstrated his instrument in relation to Hertzian waves. Popov sent his paper for publication on the same day and it was published in 1896 in Russian. However, when Marconi applied for his patent, this paper by Popov had not reached the USA. Popov's paper reached the American Academy of Sciences in Boston on 4 April 1896, eight months before Marconi had filed his patent in America. Later, Popov also accused Marconi of stealing the design of his receiver from the famous journal *The Electrician*. But then it is also true that later, Popov became a friendly enemy of Marconi and in 1902, Popov himself called Marconi the father of wireless communication. Although Russians still consider Popov the 'true father of radio communication', the same thing proves to be true in the case of Jagadish Chandra Bose as well.

In 1899, Marconi wrote, 'Science is full of examples of the wrong attribution in one of his manuscripts and it is completely absurd to talk about correcting these mistakes.' The question of originality in wireless telegraphy and the question of giving credit for the actual development work is tough to answer.

Marconi came to London from Italy in February 1896. By that time, agents for patents had become very influential in London and they had taken the form of an organization that helped the inventor get a patent by introducing him to patent lawyers and experts. On 5 March 1896, Marconi hastily applied for his patent in London by making a provisional draft. This provisional draft was of twelve pages, on which the date of February 1896 was written. This draft was written on the pages of a children's notebook in the Italian language. Most of the things in this provisional draft were not written in detail. This application was definitely very weak, but Marconi was determined to pass it.

According to the British Patent Rules, the provisional application was also considered the main basis of the patent. People would later include detailed information related to the patent. In such a situation, these papers were kept secret by the Patent Office and the candidate was given nine months in which he could collect all his patent-related information in detail. According to this rule, no machine needs to be invented to get a patent. Any person could claim its invention and take nine months to do so. Until then, it was the responsibility of the Patent Office to defend his claim. The discovery of electromagnetic waves with frequencies lower than light was similar. The invention of the instruments to discover them was claimed, but Marconi did not have a solid design of the equipment till then. On 2 June 1896, Marconi slightly improved the draft of the patent and then waited nine full months. In the meantime, he tried to protect his patent by consulting all the patent experts. Eventually, the patent for wireless telegraphy went to Marconi.

However, it is also a fact that after getting this patent, many industries began to compete to save their intellectual rights, and patenting became an important part of inventions and industrialization of technologies.

13

Praise from the Greats

The year 1895 was a crucial year for Jagadish Chandra Bose. People were astonished at his ability to create a device for transmitting and detecting microwaves with the help of simple novice carpenters and blacksmiths. The wireless transmission based on microwaves was demonstrated by Jagadish Bose in the presence of Sir Mackenzie, the then Lt Governor of Bengal, at the Town Hall of Calcutta. There should be no dispute about this.

Appreciated and pleased with his invention, Jagadish wrote a paper in 1895 on the basis of some interesting new results. Bose sent it to be published in the Journal of the Royal Society of London in 1896. It was based on measuring the 'refractive index' of sulphur and other substances for electric waves. Till now, Marconi's name was not anywhere in the world of wireless communication. Alexander Popov of Russia was undoubtedly a contemporary of Jagadish, who was having equal success in producing and detecting electromagnetic waves. The way Jagadish demonstrated these waves was by setting fire to gunpowder kept about 75 feet away and by firing pistol shots.

His mentor, Lord Rayleigh, had information about Jagadish's work in this direction. In 1895, Lord Rayleigh asked Jagadish to do some other important experiments related to modifications in his instruments. In these experiments, Jagadish introduced a unique method of measuring the wavelength of invisible electric waves. Jagadish's second paper, sent by Lord Rayleigh to the Journal of the Royal Society, was published in 1897.

Lord Rayleigh was pleased to see this result and he immediately wrote this letter back to Jagadish Bose:

* * *

Terling Place
Witham, Essex
11 November 1895
Dear Professor Bose,

I communicated your last paper to the Royal Society, and I hope it may soon be read.

It occurs to me that possibly some help might be given you for apparatus from the 'Government Grant Fund' administered by the Royal Society, or, if only a small sum (under 20 Euro) were needed from the Donation Fund.

I will ask Mr. Rix to send you a form of application in case you are disposed to try.

Yours Faithfully,
Rayleigh

* * *

This research paper brought Jagadish a high degree of respect in this field. The title of this paper was 'On the determination of the wavelength of electric radiation by diffraction grating'. Influenced by this paper of Jagadish Chandra Bose, the University of London awarded him the degree of Doctor of Science (DSc) in 1896. This rare distinction was given to Jagadish Chandra without having to appear in any formal examination. That is rare in London University's history.

The then famous English newspaper *The Englishman* of Calcutta wrote that Professor Jagadish Chandra Bose of Presidency College had created a device similar to the human eye that can also see invisible electromagnetic waves which our eyes cannot. If he completely perfects his equipment, we will see in no time that invisible waves will soon illuminate the beaches and navigating the ocean will become much more manageable. The surprising thing is that Professor Bose Chandra Bose of Presidency College himself has done this work alone without any financial help.

Meanwhile, Lord Kelvin, the famous physicist and the pioneer of thermo-physics, also wrote a letter to Jagadish Chandra Bose. Lord Kelvin had been the President of the Royal Society of London until 1895 and was respected worldwide for his contributions to physics. A unit of temperature measurement is called 'Kelvin' in his honour. He was pleased to see the research of the 39-year-old Professor Jagadish Chandra Bose and he was surprised to see how in a country like India, without any resources, an untrained youth made such an important discovery. Lord Kelvin wrote this short letter to Bose in 1896:

> *14 April 1896*
> *I thank you for your letter of March, 18th and for the exceedingly interesting pamphlet describing your experimental researches in the Physical Laboratory of your Presidency College which you have kindly sent me, and which I have received today. I have found time to look all through it, although not yet to learn all its contents, but I*

have seen enough to fill me literally with wonder and admiration, and to allow me to ask you to accept my congratulations for so much success in the difficult and novel experimental problems which you have attacked. As a slight expression of my thanks I am sending you by post, along with this, separate copies of a few papers of my own.

Kelvin
The University of Glasgow

* * *

Congratulations to Bose started pouring in from all over the world. In his own country, the British officers who did not have very good views about Indians started giving congratulatory messages. Even Sir William Croft, a staunch opponent of Jagadish Chandra Bose, congratulated him. He once said, 'Indians do not have the natural nature necessary for science.' The same Sir William Croft wrote a letter to the Government of Bengal on 16 June 1896, the excerpts of which are:

The subject dealt with has long been regarded as of very great importance, attempting as it does to the complete specification of the unknown forces involved, by determining the length of the invisible wave . . . The problem was attempted by Hertz and subsequently by a number of continental physicists but the results obtained were very contradictory. Mr Bose has recently succeeded in solving the problem with entirely satisfactory results; and a copy of the paper embodying his solution was sent to the University of London as a Thesis for the degree of Doctor of Science. I should explain that before being admitted to the examination for that degree, a candidate has to produce a Dissertation embodying the results of original research in some branch of science. On the acceptance of the Dissertation by the University, the candidate has in general

> *to undergo a further examination. There is, however, a provision in the DSc regulation that a candidate may at the discretion of the university be exempted from further examination, provided the paper submitted is of special excellence. Mr Bose received on the 27 May, a telegram from the Registrar informing him that his thesis was accepted and his presence at the examination excused . . .*

However, Jagadish Chandra Bose now wanted to travel to England to explain his invention to the then scholars himself. Discussions also open new avenues. For Jagadish's visit to Britain, Lord Rayleigh sent an invitation letter from the Royal Society, London, to the Government of Bengal and Jagadish. Referring to this letter, Sir Alfred Croft wrote in a letter to the then Governor of Bengal, William Mackenzie:

> *From the above, I hope, it will be clear that Prof. Bose is an investigator of exceptional originality and power and that he deserves all the encouragement that the Government can give him. In advocating his deputation to Europe on duty, I have in mind not merely his personal benefit, but also the resulting advantage to science.*

All the high officials of Bengal in the British government were also in favour of sending Jagadish to England. One of the reasons for this was that the officials of that time were showing at the world level and in the country how they were contributing and supporting the development of common talents of their country. In this way, on 1 July 1896, Bose's visit to England was officially announced.

> *It has been settled that Prof. Bose should proceed at once on deputation to England to be present at a meeting of the British Association.*

Prof. Bose went to England and on 21 September 1896, he gave his speech to the British Association on wireless communication and generation, transmission and detection of microwaves. Jagadish had spoken in this speech about those electromagnetic waves which were generally invisible to our eyes and we did not know anything about them. He emphasized this and said that nothing is known about the properties of these waves. He discussed the characteristics of these waves in his speech.

Lord Kelvin, J.J. Thomson, great mathematicians like Thomson, Fitzgerald, Everett, Oliver Lodge, Sir Gabriel Strokes, etc. were present. This was the professor's first speech before so many great scientists on comparatively foreign soil and he was a bit restless, but in a short time when he started talking about his work, he felt more self-confident. Bose's speech at the University of Liverpool was highly praised and he gave several addresses one after the other. The importance of his remarks was discussed, but Bose's art of giving speeches and the art of explaining the most difficult things easily was also highly praised and discussed. Newspapers published articles about Jagadish's speech.

Lord Kelvin was so impressed by Professor Bose's speech that after the speech, he jumped on the stairs leading to the women's seating area and with both hands, shook hands with Abala Bose, praising Jagadish Bose wholeheartedly.

Soon after, Professor Bose was also invited to the Royal Society, London to deliver a speech at the Royal Institute. Most importantly, he was invited to deliver a 'Friday Lecture' at the Royal Institute. 'Friday Lectures' were very famous in England and were considered honourable. They were started by Sir Michael Faraday, who was among the most important people of England who would come to the general public to listen.

When Bose informed his Indian office about this invitation, the officials there were so happy that they extended the time of his paid leave, i.e., deputation, for an additional three months. The next three months were also added to the already given leave. In this way, Professor Bose could now live comfortably in England and Europe and could take advantage of the excellent academic environment there.

Professor Jagadish Chandra Bose delivered his speech at the Royal Institute on 29 January 1897. This speech was also as successful as the Liverpool speech.

The then reputed newspaper *The Times* published the news of Professor Bose's speech the next day.

> *Last night at the Royal Institute, Professor Bose of Presidency College, Calcutta, India delivered a speech on 'The polarization of the electric rays'. Sir James Brown presided over the speech. In this speech, Lord Rayleigh, Sir Barram-Well, Professor Dewar, Professor Thomson, Fleming, Armstrong and the Simon Professors were present. This speech talked about improved versions of Hertz's instruments. Professor Bose said that he has made a better detector of his own, seeing many shortcomings in the detector named Coherer made by Professor Oliver Lodge. Chandra Bose claimed that the kind of experiments that are done with the properties of light, all such investigations should also be done for these invisible rays and his equipment is capable of doing them. He spoke about similar experiments that he had done with invisible rays.*

Apart from this, *The Electric Engineer* magazine wrote on 5 February 1897 in surprise:

> *The description of the inductive method by which Prof. Bose was led to devise his form of receiver and the reasons of its superiority to other receivers, were exceedingly interesting. It is remarkable that no secret was at any time made to the construction of his apparatus, so that it has been open to all the world to adapt it for practical and possibly money-making purposes.*

Interestingly, Marconi and Professor Preece, who worked with Marconi, met Professor Jagadish Chandra Bose in England during this trip. Jagadish Chandra Bose also discussed the parts of his equipment in detail. Prof. Bose was in favour of understanding nature through science, but he did not wish to earn money from it. He was in search of knowledge, as were all Maxwellians. At this meeting, Marconi advised Bose to get his device patented and said that if he patented it, then many of his generations would be prosperous. Bose's reply was modest and idealistic that as he is the creator of knowledge, he has no urge to earn money. In fact, by that time, Marconi had submitted only a preliminary and very rough draft of the patent for his device to the Patent Office. He had nine months to finalize the draft of his patent application as per the British Patent Manual, which was being completed in a single month. Marconi was still experimenting and had not yet finalized his instrument. Finally, on 2 March 1897, Marconi submitted the finalized draft of the patent application for his equipment and wireless communication technology to the Patent Office.

As a result, Professor Bose did not choose science to earn money as Marconi did. Marconi did not have any formal physics training nor a degree. He was an ambitious youth, only 23 years old at the time. He was the one who understood that to stay in the industry he had to learn the process of patenting correctly. Marconi took advantage of his lifelong patenting process in developing his techniques. England's patent system did not recognize the person who first made the device or developed the technology, but rather the person who first submitted the initial drafts of the technology to be invented to the Patent Office.

After the speech at the Royal Institute, Jagadish Chandra also received an invitation from the Imperial Institute to deliver a speech. Professor Bose delivered a speech at the Imperial Institute on 18 February 1897. Professor Henry Roscoe, Vice-Chancellor of the University of London, praised Professor Bose and said,

> *The brains of the East are as capable as the brains of the West in making scientific discoveries and producing experimental scientists.*

These words are going to change the discourse of the minds of the elderly. There was a sky-high difference in the salaries of English and non-English professors in Calcutta until a few years ago. These words pointed towards a bright future.

Professor Bose's last speech at the Imperial Institute was on this trip to England. At the end of Bose's tour of Europe in 1897, the Physics Councils of Paris and Berlin invited him to deliver speeches with the most respected dignitaries in Germany. After that, he left for France and Germany. The *Société de physique* speech was presided over by the famous scientist M. Carnu, who was also the President of the Academy of Science and an expert in optics and electrodynamics. These people were so excited about Bose's speech and research that he was made an honorary member of the *Société de physique*. Many scientists came from far and wide to hear Bose's speech at the Academy of Sciences in Berlin. Professor Quincke should be named among them. After coming from Heidelberg, he had come to Berlin to listen to Bose's speech. He wanted to work in Bose's research area and build the equipment made by Bose in his laboratory. He also invited Professor Bose to visit his own laboratory. Professor Warburg, the successor of Professor Helmholtz, appreciated Bose's speech in Berlin, Germany. He told another German scientist who was trying to start research in this field, '*Professor Bose has left nothing for anyone else to do in this field. It is better to try something new.*' Bose also went to the University of Kiel (where Hertz worked for some time) and also went to Professor Ebert (a well-known scientist who had worked in the field of electromagnetism) and Professor Lenard. From here he went back to India via Heidelberg at Professor Quincke's place. Thus, passing through Europe, Professor Bose returned to India again. He received a grand welcome in Calcutta.

As soon as the people of Calcutta got word of the return of Jagadish Chandra Bose, people thronged the Howrah railway station to welcome their hero. It is said that there was such a crowd at the Howrah railway station that day that there was a stampede.

People invited Jagadish Chandra Bose for several days to different institutions to welcome him back home. After some time, on 19 July 1897, Rabindranath Tagore went to Jagadish Chandra Bose's house to meet and congratulate him. Coincidentally, Bose was not at home that day and he did not reach home even after a long wait. Then, Rabindranath Tagore brought a bunch of Magnolia flowers as a gift and left it with a self-written poem for Bose. The poem which Tagore wrote for Bose in Bengali, is as follows:

Across the seas, on the Western Ghats,
of the prosperity of science
The temple of the goddess reigns.
There you have travelled my friend,
And you have come back from there wearing a crown.
You have crowned your motherland
One who is humble, poor and shy at heart.
Remote lands
Great and successful people
Unitedly praised your work
His words resonate as his message
Across the seas, far and wide

Her eyes are full of tears
Mother with your humble heart
Sending blessings
Through a poet

Never heard of in the world of science
These words in your ears
Mother's sweet whisper
In the sound of
Will reverberate

It had been a long time since Rabindranath Tagore and Bose became friends. Tagore was taking care of his ancestral property while living in Shilaidaha, which is now in Bangladesh. While living here, Tagore wrote his story collection *Galp-Guchchh*, containing eighty-four stories.

Bose and Tagore were good friends for life. Bose gave Tagore a scientific outlook and Tagore gave Bose the sentiments of a poet or artist. Both were almost the same age, Tagore being about two and half years younger than Bose.

In the same year, in 1897, Alfred Carnu, former president of the French Academy of Sciences, also wrote a letter to Jagadish Chandra Bose, congratulating and praising him. He wrote:

> *Your first research results validate your ability to advance scientific progress. At my level, I hope to take full advantage of the usefulness of the ideal tool made by you in my further experiments and for the betterment of further research at Ecole Polytechnic.*

Even though it appears that Jagadish had got his scientific breakthrough in a very short time, if you look carefully, it will be found that this is contrary to the truth. Jagadish Chandra Bose's training and dedication from childhood until then was also to be included. Jagadish was a big proponent of having a workshop to make the equipment needed for his scientific experiments. He was able to make such sensitive tools with a novice blacksmith and carpenter because, in his childhood, he had seen and understood the process of making parts by visiting the workshop set up by his father. Even after this, he continued to demonstrate to the students in his class at Presidency College the general versions of the instruments designed by Hertz to generate and detect low-frequency electromagnetic waves so that they could be anywhere in the world at the time. He was well-aware of scientific discoveries taking place. This was why he did not take much time to succeed in his research work.

Although the London newspaper *Spectator* continuously published negative and critical news about academic activities and science-related activities in the Indian and Eastern countries. But out of curiosity, the editor of this newspaper reached the Royal Institute to hear Jagadish Chandra Bose's speech and he was so impressed that he later praised Jagadish in his newspaper. An excerpt from this article, published a few weeks after the speech, in the *Spectator*:

> *There is however, to our thinking, something of a rare interest in the spectacle there presented, of a Bengalee of the purest dsecent lecturing in London to an audience of appreciative European savants upon one of the most recondite branches of modern physical science. It suggests at least the possibility that we may one day see an invaluable addition to the great army of those who are trying by acute observation and patient experimentation to wring from Nature some of her most jealously guarded secrets. The people of the East have just the burning imagination which could extort a truth out of a mass of apparently disconnected facts—a habit of meditation without allowing the mind to dissipate itself, such as has belonged to the greatest mathematicians and engineers—and a power of persistence—it is something a little different from patience—such as hardly belong to any European. We do not know Professor Bose—but we venture to say that if he caught with his scientific imagination a glimpse of a wonder-working*

'ray' as yet unknown to man but always penetrating ether and believed that experiment would reveal its properties and potentialities, he would go on experimenting ceaselessly through a long life and dying, hand on his task to some successor, be it son or be it a disciple. Nothing would seem laborious to him in his enquiry, nothing insignificant, nothing painful, any more than it would seem to the true sanyasi in the pursuit of his inquiry into the ultimate relation of his own spirit to that of the Divine. Just think what kind of addition to the means of investigation would be made by the arrival within that sphere of inquiry of a thousand men with the sanyasi mind, the mind which utterly controls the body and can meditate and inquire endlessly while life remains, never for a moment losing sight of the object, never for a moment letting it be obscured by any terrestrial temptation.

We can see no reason whatever why the Asiatic mind, turning from its absorption in insoluble problems, should not betake itself ardently, thirstily, hungrily, the research into Nature which can never end, yet is always yielding results, often evil as well as good, upon which yet deeper enquiries can be based. If that happened—and Professor Bose is at all events living evidence that it can happen—that would be the greatest addition ever made to the sum of mental force of mankind.

The Times newspaper wrote:

The originality of the achievement is enhanced by the fact that Dr Bose had to do the work in addition to his incessant duties as Professor of Physical Science in Calcutta and with apparatus and appliances which in this country would be deemed altogether inadequate. He had to construct himself his instruments as he went along. His work forms the outcome of his twofold lines of labour—construction and research.

Meanwhile, Lord Lister (the then President of the Royal Society), Lord Kelvin, Professor Clifton, Professor Fitzgerald, Professor Pointing, Sir William Ramsay, Sir Gabriel Stocks, Professor S. Thompson and other intellectuals sent a letter of appreciation to the Secretary of State of India, which read:

> *. . . to the great importance, which we attach to the establishment in the Indian Empire of a Central Laboratory for advanced teaching and research in connection with the Presidency College, Calcutta. We believe that it would be not only beneficial in respect to higher education, but also that it would largely promote the material interest of the country—and we venture to urge on you the desirability of establishing in India a Physical Laboratory worthy of that great Empire.*

Meanwhile, Lord Kelvin from England wrote a letter to Lord Hamilton, Secretary to the Government of India, praising Bose.

> *It would be conducive to the credit of India and the scientific education in Calcutta, if a well-equipped physical laboratory is added to the resources of University of Calcutta in connection with the Professorship held by Dr Bose.*

Impressed by this, the Secretary of State of India wrote this to the Government of India in May 1897:

> *Being of the opinion that the question of establishing an institution of the kind mentioned is deserving of consideration by Your Excellency in the Council . . .*

The then Viceroy Lord Elgin told Bose that the Government of India was taking an interest in the task and may have told the Government of Bengal about it. Through all the departments, it came to be known that notes have been put out to say that this scheme is important but can be postponed for the future. Bose understood this. He convinced the government on the importance of his scientific work but it was difficult to convince the departmental machinery. Although his well-wishers living in England wanted to see this plan completed as soon as possible, Bose understood that he would have to leave his work for a long time and sit idle if he waited for it. Therefore, he decided that he would continue his research in the old conditions only.

Returning from England in 1897, Bose resumed his regular duties in the Presidency College. About two months after his return to the country, he made a proposal to give financial assistance to the Government of India. In response to which the remarks written to him by a member of the Finance Department on 7 September 1897 are noteworthy:

> *He (Bose) is now drawing Rs 500 and it is simple nonsense on the part of a native gentleman in the service of the Government to talk, under such circumstances of 'difficulty in maintaining himself on his small means'. I wonder what any of the Universities in England would say to any of his staff who said, 'I am a distinguished man, and you must agree to give me, on that account, more than the allowance of my offices.' I think Mr Bose has got his head a bit turned and can wait a bit for his distinctions and records.*

However, the Home Member of the British government (who later became the Governor) acknowledged Bose's demands:

> *Mr Bose's distinction is not any ordinary distinction and so as to the adequacy of his salary, I am personally aware that it has not been sufficient to meet the expenses of his experiments and tours . . .*

Even in the Presidency College, many colleagues were not happy with Bose's success and his sudden rise and started feeling jealous of him. In the meantime, the headmaster of the Presidency College, who had been helping Bose in the best possible way, retired. The education department directors, who gave consideration to Bose's work, had also changed. The new headmaster of the Presidency College was jealous of Bose's work and progress. Now, Professor Bose was starting to get a more hostile atmosphere at the college level. Every tedious task in the college would often be sent to Prof. Bose to distract him from research. College officials and senior professors said that the main job of a professor is to teach the students and the professors should concentrate all their attention on teaching. Jagadish was given twenty-six hours of classes a week and these included demonstrations of experiments. This teaching time was much longer than that of his fellow professors, but they all kept criticizing Bose. They tried to prove all the time that Professor Bose was not able to do his teaching job properly and that he was not serious about his responsibilities.

Along with teaching the classes, Bose would finish the other tasks given by the college on time and then get more and more tired. He carried on his research work late in the evening or at night, at whatever time he got. He had neither any financial assistance nor the general support of any person and everything had to be done alone. With his limited salary and hard work, he was able to keep his research alive.

Meanwhile, the memorandum was sent to the Secretary of India with the signatures of almost all the scientists present at the speech of Jagadish Chandra Bose at the British Association. Thus, the then Secretary of India and Viceroy of India, Lord Elgin, was put under a lot of pressure by the British scientists.

The effect of this pressure was not so much that a high-class laboratory could be opened under the leadership of Bose, but the result of these letters and memorandums from England was that

Jagadish Chandra Bose came into the eyes of the country's leading officials. The then Lieutenant Governor of Bengal, Charles Stevens, was greatly influenced by the work of Jagadish Bose. He was well aware of the condition of the universities in India. He was aware of the rotten education system in the country. In such a situation, he was also aware of the difficulties in their own institutions of those who follow a logical and positive learning method for the progress of knowledge. He wanted to help Bose. Charles Stevens thought of creating a new post for Jagadish Chandra Bose, which would be more remunerative and where he could mainly do research work. The main task of the officer in this post would be to develop research laboratories in all the government colleges affiliated with the universities of Bengal. He could prepare the students to solve advanced science problems and teach them to be educators, so that young students learn to think independently. This new plan was passed and Bose was told that soon he would get an official letter in this regard. But due to the politics and deviousness of the university and education department, it failed in the end.

In those days, Bose used to be a Fellow of the University of Calcutta, which was aided by the government but used to be an independent institution to a large extent. There were many fellows at the university from whom Bose's views on many issues used to be completely different. The University of Calcutta was in the role of the nodal centre in the new scheme under which Bose was to be appointed to the new post. A few days before the appointment letter of Bose was prepared, a meeting of the fellows of the University of Calcutta was held in which a decision was to be taken regarding a serious issue. Bose's views were different from those of other fellows, so when voting took place on this issue too, Jagadish's vote was opposed to other people's views. This protest deeply hurt the pride of the head of the fellow members of the university, who were very senior professors. He could not understand how a young and new professor was cut off from his senior professor. That too, in front of the general public! Due to his influence, the appointment of Professor Bose to the new post was cancelled. In this way, that plan was also stalled. The University of Calcutta had to play the leading role in the implementation of this scheme and in the end, the university administration refused to take responsibility.

Professor Bose was deeply shocked by this incident. He was also sad and angry for a long time. In the meantime, on another occasion, a letter came from the Secretary of the Government to Jagadish, asking for an explanation from him for attending an important meeting of the fellow members of the University of Calcutta (at which an important issue was to be decided). Bose could not attend the meeting for some other reason, but the clarification that was sought made him angry. Bose wrote an equally bold letter in reply. He asked clearly in the letter if in the university meetings, the government wants to pass the views of the people put forward by them without any opposition and wants the junior people to keep their votes aside. Do the people put forward by the government blindly become hangers? Suppose the government considers his 'inability to perform his assigned duties' to exercise his free thought and vote. In that case, he (Bose) would like to request that he be allowed to resign from the Fellowship of the University of Calcutta. Jagadish's case escalated and was eventually transferred to the lieutenant governor. The lieutenant governor was aware of Jagadish's capabilities and conscientiousness and wanted him to take over his new post but could not do anything in favour of Jagadish due to opposition from the education department. Jagadish's opponent from the education department was so intense that the lieutenant governor was helpless in front of him.

However, Lieutenant Governor Charles Stevens really wanted to help Bose in every way possible. He could not help Bose in the previous case, so he thought of helping Professor Bose in another way. He proposed by writing a letter to Bose that he wanted to return the enormous expenditure incurred on the research of Professor Bose to him on behalf of the government. He wanted Bose to tell him in detail about the expenses incurred in research so far and then he wanted to give that money back to Bose from the government. But Bose flatly refused to accept any help from the government for the previous research, although he respected the offer of help by the lieutenant governor. Jagadish wanted the government to help him with his future research. Therefore, the government recommended annual financial assistance of 166 euros, or about 2500 rupees, which was to be spent on the future research of Bose in the Presidency College.

In this way, Professor Bose got some financial help from the government, but his problems at the college level were not lessening. The burden of teaching the students kept increasing on him. The management of the college would make every effort to harass him in other ways as well.

In 1897–98, the world-famous physicist and guru of Jagadish Chandra Bose in Cambridge, Lord Rayleigh, along with his wife, visited India via America and Egypt. One of the primary reasons for his coming to India was a total solar eclipse visible from India, which he wanted to see. Lord Rayleigh also thought it appropriate to visit Jagadish Chandra Bose's laboratory, taking advantage of this visit. Jagadish Chandra Bose also happily took his guru to Presidency College to see the laboratory, which he had built in his sitting room. Lord Rayleigh explained his research work in detail to Jagadish and the two had a long conversation. Although Lord Rayleigh was familiar with Jagadish's research work as much as he had shown him in London, a lot of it was new. Lord Rayleigh saw Jagadish's equipment in detail and Jagadish learned a lot from Lord Rayleigh. It all went well, but surprisingly, on his way home from the laboratory in the evening itself, Professor Bose got a memorandum from the college principal asking him for immediate clarification.

> *I learnt from Lord Rayleigh that he visited the Presidency College this morning and inspected the laboratory which he was shown by you. I should be glad to hear by what authority you have received outsiders into the Laboratory.*

All this was happening every day with Prof. Jagadish in the Presidency College. However, Bose's research work continued in the meantime and he sent some more papers for publication.

14

Struggle Continues

In 1865, just seven years after the birth of Jagadish Chandra Bose, a young Scottish scientist, James Clerk Maxwell, published a research paper in the journal *Philosophical Transactions of the Royal Society* called 'A Dynamical Theory of the Electromagnetic Field'. This paper put Maxwell on par with Newton in the history of science. In this research, Maxwell proved on a theoretical basis that the electric and magnetic fields in the wave form are counterparts to each other and that both change together and move at the speed of light into infinity. Maxwell's theoretical formulas gave a new direction to modern electromagnetism. Theoretically, Maxwell's laws also meant that, like light, electromagnetic waves should exist whose wavelengths would be shorter and longer than those of light and that they may not be visible. Light waves have long piqued scientists' interest and they continue to do so in the twenty-first century. According to Maxwell, an infinite range of waves must exist in which visible light is only a window or a tiny part of that spectrum. Scientists were engaged in generating these unknown waves and wanted to know about the characteristics of these waves. But being beyond light, everything was in darkness.

To generate these invisible waves, it needed equipment and divine eyes to see them.

Maxwell died in 1879 at the age of 48. He loved to write poems. A great lover of Scottish poetry, Maxwell remembered all the poems he sang while playing his guitar. In 1882, his friend, Lewis Campbell, published a collection of poems by Maxwell. Maxwell's theories were as deep, detailed and poetic as his poems. The year Maxwell died in England, Heinrich Hertz worked with Gustav Kirchhoff and Hermann von Helmholtz for a PhD from the University of Berlin, Germany. After receiving his PhD from the University of Berlin in 1880, Heinrich Hertz did postdoctoral work with Helmholtz for the next three years, before becoming a lecturer in theoretical physics at the University of Kiel, Germany. In 1885, he was awarded the title of full professor by the University of Karlsruhe, Germany.

During his tenure at the University of Kiel, Hertz presented a variety of analyses of Maxwell's theories, showing that the validity of Maxwell's laws was greater than was thought of at the time. After coming to the University of Karlsruhe, he started experimenting with theoretical physics in the year 1886. These can be considered the epoch-making moments in the history of physics that prepared the world to achieve new technological heights. Hertz gave us new eyes to see the world through new waves beyond the reach of light. This was possible because Hertz already had a better theoretical understanding of Maxwell's laws.

It was necessary to periodically produce electric vibrations to generate electric waves which had to be of the same amplitude. The frequency of these vibrations would be very high and hence control over the instrument was also necessary. Hertz succeeded in doing this after a lot of effort. The production of vibrations was done between two copper balls with an electric discharge between them. But that was not enough. The biggest challenge was determining whether the vibrations produced by these electric discharges were the same waves that Maxwell had proposed. To do this, a precise receiver was needed, which would be able to accept these waves. After much trouble with this, Hertz tried many processes and finally succeeded with one. He placed two metallic sticks very close together and tried to induce electric tension. Initially, he did not receive any induced electric current. Hertz knew that the magnitude of this induced electric current would be minimal. Hertz was able to receive these invisible waves with the help of his receiver. It was a historic moment in the world of science. Another window had opened to see the world; a new world that could be seen through the invisible light.

However, it was only the beginning. Much investigation was yet to be done to prove that these electric vibrations were a type of Maxwellian wave. Students of science studied the characteristics of the waves. In addition to this, these waves were to display all the attributes of Maxwellian or electromagnetic waves.

Now, it was necessary to have a detailed look at the vibrations generated by Hertz. Wavelength is one of the most important characteristics of waves. The smallest waves produced by Hertz had a wavelength of about 4 metres, and the largest waves had a wavelength of a few 100 metres. It also proved that the spectrum of electromagnetic waves could spread over a large distance, both above and below the spectrum of light. Now, the question was, do these waves behave like light? That is, can these invisible waves pass through something, or is an object opaque to them? Do they also show the known properties of light like reflection, refraction, diffusion, diffraction, polarization, etc.?

Hertz wanted to repeat Newton's famous experiment for waves of light with prisms for his invisible waves instead to see how they behaved. The scholars of science knew that if light rays are emitted through a prism, they bend towards the prism's base. What if these extremely long-wavelength, invisible, electric waves were passed through a prism? This might sound simple, but it was not. Since the wavelengths of these waves ranged from a few metres to a few hundred metres, experiments with them would have required a wide prism at least a few metres long. Where do you get such large glass prisms?

Hertz did not give up. He made a giant prism by casting a few tonnes of glass and experimented with it. As expected, when these rays turned towards the base of the prism, Hertz's experiment was successful. It meant that these rays were obeying the laws of refraction like light. After the success of this experiment, Hertz became very excited and started thinking about doing further experiments. He also conducted polarization experiments with these invisible waves. Such large waves also required equipment like giant polarizers and analyzers, which were a major challenge to make. The smallest invisible waves produced by Hertz were also a few metres in wavelength. After much difficulty, Hertz proved the polarization of these waves by using giant gratings made of metallic grids. In this way, it was established that these invisible waves are a kind of Maxwellian wave. However, it was very difficult or even impossible to do other experiments with these waves with any kind of precision and accuracy. The biggest reason for this was their huge wavelength.

After years of hard work and lack of attention to his health, Hertz became seriously ill at a very young age. However, it was not that it was a fatal disease. Hertz started having migraine attacks and problems with nasal catarrh. During this treatment, Hertz died in 1894 in Bonn (Germany) at the age of only 36, due to the worsening of a minor surgery and the resultant infection. Through Hertz, science had much to discover and it was an irreparable loss.

However, it was in 1894 that Jagadish Chandra Bose set out on a new path in his life to do research. Along with Bose, other scientists from around the world were working on this project, of which Oliver Lodge was an important part. At that time, generating waves of different wavelengths of invisible electric waves was becoming prevalent and people were into their characteristics.

From 1895 to 1897, Jagadish Chandra Bose did a lot of work on such kinds of invisible electric waves. The most important challenge of the time was to generate invisible electric waves of various wavelengths. It was also necessary to study the light-related characteristics of these invisible waves accurately. If the wavelength is shorter, the equipment needed to study the waves will also be smaller and relatively easier to build.

The most important work of Jagadish Chandra Bose was also to generate invisible waves of short-wavelengths. The invisible waves he managed to produce were a few millimetres in wavelength. Experimenting with them was more straightforward and better than the waves generated by Hertz to obtain accurate experimental results.

In the early days, Bose produced electric waves with a wavelength of 66 cm. However, it was not easy to test the polarization characteristics for these waves as well because it was not easy to make such large polarizers and analyzers. Bose then faced the challenge of producing invisible electric waves of even shorter wavelengths. After many efforts, Bose finally successfully generated invisible electric waves of 5 millimetres wavelength. He created a new radiator device that was more precise and subtle. Simultaneously, Bose studied the polarization effect in these millimetre electric waves. The instruments made by Bose were fundamentally different from those made by Hertz. It was impossible to produce and study such small waves with Hertz's methods. Bose also measured air, water, glass and sulphur refractive indices for his waves. All these experiments were carried out with utmost precision. Thus, it was proved that the invisible waves of millimetre-wavelength produced by Bose, which people called electric waves, were electromagnetic waves as proposed by Maxwell. In the process, Bose also created his own detector, which he called 'the Coherer'. Scientists around the world praised 'the Coherer' made by Bose with the help of a spiral spring. It was a modified form of a simple device made by the famous scientist Branly.

In 1897, Lord Rayleigh published a theoretical paper in very reputed journal called the *Philosophical Magazine* in which he discussed the scientific aspects regarding the flow of these invisible electric waves in a cylindrical (dielectric) wire. It is said that the inspiration to do such scientific work came from listening to the speech given by Bose to the British Association. It was the beginning of important research regarding the flow of modes in waveguides. This research can be called the foundation stone of today's 'optical fibres'. Optical fibres are those with which most of the communication happens today across the globe.

In the same year, six papers of Jagadish Chandra Bose were published, out of which four were published in the *Proceedings of the Royal Society*. One research paper was published in the prestigious *Philosophical Magazine* and one in *Friday Evening Discourse* given at the Royal Institution of London. The first paper of 1897 was about the measurement of the wavelength of electric radiation by diffraction grating. In this research paper, the method of measuring the wavelength of invisible electric waves was proved under a new process different from the receiver made by Hertz. Before this, only Hertz's receivers could measure the wavelengths of these waves in the air. Its biggest drawback was that the design of this receiver affected the experiments being done, so it could not make accurate measurements. Bose invented a process in which the measurement of wavelengths of invisible radiation in free space was not affected by the design of the receiver. For this, he used Roland's Curve Grating Process. Bose explained his entire device in detail in this paper. He used his indigenous radiator and spiral spring receiver in this process. In the discussion of this paper, Professor Bose wrote that with the use of this instrument, the wavelength of invisible waves could be measured with great accuracy. He also wrote in this paper that he was trying to improve this device even more and would soon send a new paper about it. This research paper, published in the *Proceedings of the Royal Society*, was examined and sent by Lord Rayleigh himself for publication.

In his following paper, Bose wrote about the design of a full-fledged instrument to study the various characteristics of electric waves and sent it to be published in the *Philosophical Magazine*. In this paper, he proved the observance of the laws of reflection, refraction, diffraction and polarization in invisible electric waves like optical rays. For these experiments, he used different types of mirrors, prisms, gratings, polarizing crystals, electro-polariscopes and polarimeters, etc. In this research, giving a detailed description of his entire device, he described his experiments related to reflection, refraction, absorption, interference and polarization with invisible electric rays.

In the next paper, he demonstrated the special selective electrical conductivity of polarizing crystals. He demonstrated this in various crystals like nemalite, chrysotile, etc. After this, his research journey continued as he measured the refractive index of glass and other materials for invisible electric waves. Jagadish Chandra Bose also demonstrated the phenomenon of 'complete internal reflection' by these invisible waves, which was a very important experiment. The accuracy and precision of all these experiments were of a very high order. The year 1897 was scientifically very successful for Bose.

In 1898, Professor Bose again published a paper in the *Proceedings of the Royal Society*, which later opened a new path. He explained the behaviour of sugar molecules inside sugar water solution by studying the polarization of invisible waves with the help of bundles of jute threads. Bose designed the bundles of jute threads in such a way that they could be easily twisted and thus, he wanted to imitate the behaviour of sugar molecules in solution. It proved to be the first step toward microwave modelling of molecular processes and Bose opened a new field of science to the world. Bose published another important paper about electromagnetic radiation in the journal *Proceedings of the Royal Society*.

Bose continued to improve the equipment he had created. For a better communication system, high-quality equipment, i.e., radiators and receivers, were needed. Bose further improved some of the receivers already available, also known as coherers. Back then, people only knew only about good conductors and bad conductors of electricity and were unaware of semiconductors. When quantum mechanics had not even come into existence, Jagadish Chandra Bose had done some experiments on semiconductors. He observed that coherers filled with metallic substances deteriorate very quickly and made efforts to improve the Coherer. During these efforts, he made a 'single point contact' with a metallic plate, thereby greatly increasing the sensitivity of the detector. He then measured the current at different voltages and contact pressure points. He found that different substances behave as two—positive and negative. By injecting invisible radiation into some substances, the electric current flow reduces in some, while increasing in some others. It was a different behaviour from Coherer's early theories. Professor Bose's scholarship and patience helped him design and test several single-point contact devices.

When Bose experimented with Galena, he found that it could detect the entire electromagnetic spectrum between violet and millimetre waves. Jagadish Chandra Bose called it the 'electric eye' because it detected invisible radiation. Bose patented this 'electric eye'. Later in 1955, two scientists named

Pearson and Brattain wrote that Bose's materials in his 'electric eye' were 'semiconductor' materials/crystals. Brattain is the same scientist who, along with Schockley and Bardeen, later won the Nobel Prize for discovering the transistor. It took half a century for the materials used by Bose to be rediscovered and used. Bose may not have used the word 'semiconductor' for these particular substances, but he knew that he had discovered a different type of material. Bose was doing all this with the help of self-made instruments in a small self-made laboratory of a college in a colonial country. He was doing all of this while fulfilling his teaching, administration and other responsibilities. The most important thing is that he was alone while doing all this. He was studying these different types of materials to improve his detector. If he had the time and cooperation, he might have studied these semiconductors in detail and the world would not have to wait several decades for semiconductors to be discovered.

Due to the humid weather of Bengal, many metal particles used in the receiver got oxidized. In addition, receivers made by other scientists such as Branly, Oliver Lodge, etc., lost their ability while working and had to be stimulated to restart. In this way, while exploring the substances, Jagadish Chandra Bose found a Coherer that would automatically recover. He sent a paper 'On Self-Recovering Coherer' to the *Proceedings of Royal Society*, which was also published. Bose observed that the efficiency of these Coherers/receivers starts decreasing due to continuous work for a long time. He found this to be an exciting phenomenon. He had seen humans getting tired, but do machines get tired too? He studied fatigue in machines using different materials. He called it exhaustion because these substances regained their functionalities over time. After many decades, today, the research area of fatigue in substances has become very important. Scientists in the twenty-first century from all over the world work in this field to identify the efficiency of machines and avoid accidents.

Bose coined and defined terms such as 'electric touch' and 'contact sensation' to understand these scientific phenomena better. In this process, he investigated and tested the effect of invisible electric waves on all metals and found that different metals in the periodic table of elements are affected differently by electric waves; some are more sensitive and some less.

Bose also tried photography with these invisible electric waves and took some photographs without using light. He found that the chemicals used in this type of photography (the developer and the photographic plate) must be differently sensitive to the chemicals required for the rays of light.

Another important event took place in 1897 which created an upheaval in physics. This event was the discovery of the electron. Professor J.J. Thomson of England discovered the electron. Thomson was the *Guru-Bhai* of Jagadish Chandra Bose. Both did their initial research under the direction of Lord Rayleigh. J.J. Thomson's initial experiments toward the discovery of the electron were successful in April 1897. He discovered some interesting properties of asymmetric cathode rays.

In that era, on the one hand, there was a struggle to find waves with a frequency lower than light, while on the other hand, scientists were also in competition to find electromagnetic waves with a frequency higher than light. In this effort, in 1895, Wilhelm Röntgen discovered X-rays. He was awarded the Nobel Prize in 1901 for the discovery of X-rays made on 8 November 1895. He had generated and detected these electromagnetic waves at that time and he recorded these waves on a film of barium platinocyanide. Röntgen called these rays 'X-rays' because he did not know much about the properties of these rays.

In 1899, Jagadish Chandra Bose sent a letter to his friend Rabindranath Tagore, which is as follows:

Friday
Dear friend,
In order to find ray of light in darkness, I am on the verge of blindness due to the intense glare of light. I will speak to you a few words on this subject when we meet. I hope, you all (including Loken and Suren) will be coming on Sunday by eight/nine in the morning. Now, it is your turn, please, bring that form. You have to meditate because I may have a difference of opinion with Judge Sahib and that may fall upon the verdict.

If possible, please, come via Presidency College at 8 AM. A patient had fractured his back. He has to be examined by the Röntgen Machine. You may say that his is not a serious disease. Because, in this country, like malaria, this too has become rampant. I have also said the same thing but could not refuse the request of Dr Nilratan Sarkar.

If you cannot come via college, please, reach 85, Upper Circular Road directly, at nine. I shall be back by that time.

Yours,
Jagadish Chandra Bose

In this letter, an X-ray machine is being discussed, which was assembled by Jagadish Chandra Bose in his laboratory at that time. Dr Nilratan Sarkar was a well-known physician of that time and the Vice-Chancellor of the University of Calcutta. It is believed that this letter was written in February 1899, although no date was written on it.

Bose had no choice but to prepare the equipment himself, spending money out of his pocket. But still, he was able to do it somehow. In college, the workload of teaching and other academic activities kept increasing and people kept trying so that Bose would not have time for research after daily activities. Meanwhile, the confrontation between Bose and the office bearers of the Presidency College continued. When Bose got fed up of the college's non-cooperation and realized that his research would not be possible while staying in Calcutta, he again wrote a letter to the lieutenant governor. He requested the lieutenant governor that he should be allowed to go to Europe first. He should be given a year's leave to work with the scientists of Europe and complete his old work. Though the lieutenant governor had great respect for Jagadish Bose's talent and understood his conditions at Presidency, he could not do anything for Bose alone. He wrote a letter to Bose and asked whether such an expensive foreign trip would prove to be an injustice? Bose felt very bad after getting this answer. He wrote another letter in response, again asking the lieutenant governor whether the government could send him to England on a scientific deputation basis. The lieutenant governor replied that the government does not send Indian officers to England by deputation for educational matters alone, but he would make some efforts. The lieutenant governor also mentioned in the counter letter that the Board of Education meeting held in Shimla had passed a resolution that despite all the government's efforts, the educational institutions of India do not perform well in scientific discoveries. After reading this, Bose once again felt like he was being cheated. Until a few days ago, his research was ringing worldwide and in just a few days, he had to read such letters.

Jagadish was finally called to Darjeeling for an interview on scientific deputation to England. When Jagadish met the lieutenant governor in this interview, Jagadish put all that was in his mind in very clear words before the lieutenant governor. The lieutenant governor was so uncomfortable with Jagadish's harsh words, which he put forward amid many people, that he adjourned the interview. He was not at all happy with Jagadish's negativity.

Disappointed once more, Jagadish came back the next day from Darjeeling to Calcutta. Just as he was about to step into the train compartment, he was given a letter from the Director of Public Instruction. It said that the Governor has proposed to send Jagadish Bose on scientific deputation to England on his own responsibility for the next six months. Jagadish can start his Europe trip whenever he wants. It was also written in this letter that the Governor's office will send a telegram to Jagadish in detail about it. The Lieutenant Governor will personally liaise with the Government of India and the Secretary to the Government in London in this direction. The Director of Public Instruction also wrote in praise of Bose:

> *Dr Bose's work is not merely the education of candidates for university degrees, but the promotion of physical science in a line which he has made peculiarly his own. To help him in that is to promote the cause of science all over the world which, I assume, falls within the functions of government.*

The Lieutenant Governor had also added in his recommendation letter that he had done whatever he could to encourage the research of Dr Bose and that he thinks that a great government should do so as well when it has a man of the highest merit among its employees. He strongly supported Bose's visit to England and his spending time and learning in the company of the greatest people in the field of science.

Going abroad again was not an easy decision. Jagadish Chandra Bose had fought a long time for this. Earlier, Bose had received an invitation to participate in a scientific congress to be held in Paris.

15

The Great Friendship

Jagadish Chandra Bose and Rabindranath Tagore had become good friends by now. Rabindranath Tagore used to send Bose his poems before they were published and shared his literary ambitions with him. Jagadish Chandra Bose also used to share his life and science issues with Rabindranath Tagore. There was regular correspondence between Bose and Rabindranath Tagore. In the early 1900s, Jagadish Chandra Bose wrote this letter to Rabindranath Tagore, opening the mysteries of his mind:

* * *

85, Lower Circular Road
2 March 1900
Dear friend,

. . . . . .

I had been to Belvedere last Tuesday. Sir J. Woodburn had always been gracious and benevolent to me. He expressed his deep satisfaction in my work and his eagerness to visit the laboratory to see the ongoing experiments and talk to my students on the next

Monday. You all had opined that I ought to attend the Paris Congress. Finding his interest in my work, I told him of your view and also mentioned the invitation I had received. The Lt. Governor assured me of all help but the Secretary of State was empowered to give the ultimate nod.

I was very enthusiastic the whole of last week and the experiment has successfully been accomplished today itself. At the same moment I received a letter from the Director-

'I have been informed that you had an interview with the Lt. Governor and have asked to be deputed to the Paris Exhibition to attend a meeting of European Scientists. May I ask you to inform me of the reasons for making your request to His Honour.'

I do not know what explanation I should give for my inordinate ambition.

The ultimate results of our deeds are many and again many an unfulfilled aspiration lead to our miseries in every step of our life.

How much mean-hearted do we have to be and how narrow should we make our periphery of work—where is the end of it?

I could not help but write to you all these, knowing fully well that you will be afflicted. I know not when and what sort of unforeseen downfall awaits me.

It would be better if the matter is not leaked out. One thing more. It would have been even better if I were ignorant of the fact that you had taken an interest in me because I won't be able in case any information is sought after. It is ignominious for the govt. to appreciate the existence of any laboratory other than the government's own. I do not dare to even think of the torture which I will be subjected to. Once, I used to cherish the dream of doing many a good work, but all my hopes are now shattered.

I expect to work on many subjects, but all have now become so knotty that I doubt if I will ever be able to unite those.

However, I will remember your affection and that will remain as my greatest reward.

You are going to Tripura. Tender my reverence to Maharaja.

I would have come along but for my leave.

I shall send you a sample of the crossbred fruit, please show that to Maharaja.

Yours,
Jagadish Chandra Bose

* * *

In a letter to his close friend and famous Bengali intellectual, Rabindranath Tagore, Jagadish had poured out his deep despair and sorrow. Such despair, in the mind of a person whose last few years have been very successful, was disturbing. Sometime after, this brought turmoil in the life of Jagadish Chandra Bose.

Jagadish and Tagore's friendship was now beginning to mature. They shared their joys and sorrows. Jagadish listened to Tagore's songs, poems and stories. It is said that Bose always read something before going to sleep, in which Tagore's poems were his favourite. Bose had always considered himself very close to the character of Karna in the Mahabharata since childhood. Karna did not want anything for himself in life. He always donated whatever he could. Bose also did not want anything for himself and did not keep anything for himself. It is said that it was Bose who inspired Tagore to write a poem on Kunti and Karna (Spring 1900). After this, Tagore wrote the poem *Karn-Kunti Samvad* (Karn-Kunti Dialogue). Bose was not involved in the freedom struggle against the British. He was working in a government institution under the British, but he was devoted to the cause of his country. Karna did not go with the Pandavas and fight against the Kauravas. Karna had nothing but had to sacrifice everything.

Amid this dismay, he heard that the Lieutenant Governor, Sir J. Woodburn, was visiting the Presidency College laboratory to see his experiments. Woodburn, the Lieutenant Governor of Bengal, was quite satisfied to see his laboratory. He was delighted and excited to learn and understand the experiments in Bose's laboratory. He was happy and expressed his desire to provide a scholarship of Rs 100/- to a student of Jagadish Chandra Bose for three years. The selection of the student would be based on the nomination of Professor Bose. After seeing all this, the Principal of Presidency College was very surprised and it was now his compulsion to show his generosity in front of Bose. Bose was surprised to see the changed behaviour of the principal. After this, Bose received a letter from the Director of Public Instruction:

> *You misunderstood me. The Governor intends to send you to Paris and wants me to send a report in this regard. I want to discuss this matter with you.*

Jagadish Chandra Bose went to meet the Director the next day. The Director was behaving in a very formal manner at first, but he gradually became liberal. When Professor Bose explained his experiments in detail, he said:

> *These are too surprising. I would like to be at your laboratory along with a couple of my friends. I want to show them all. When will it be convenient for you?*

The Director accepted that Bose's experiments were very important. Bose found the director's behaviour very encouraging at that time and he saw the problem solved. But when Professor Bose reminded the director about going to Paris, the director's behaviour changed and he asked Bose if he could go to Paris later.

This question was the best hint to postpone Bose's request. The director also told Bose:

> *The only difficulty is that there is no one who can take up your work during your absence, the college will suffer.*

The Director continued to speak and Bose listened silently as he remembered his last foreign visit. The classes had gone on smoothly, which was well known to the Director. He was pretending to be ignorant. The Director then asked Bose to hand over the invitation letter he had received from Paris to send a report to the Governor. Jagadish became more upset at this. In a letter, Jagadish Chandra Bose wrote to his integral friend Rabindranath Tagore (6 March 1900):

> *I feel ashamed to tell you that the letter of invitation remains missing. I was carrying it in my pocket for days altogether and perhaps the shirt has gone for laundry for a wash! You can well understand the deplorable mental state of mine. I told him that I could produce a new letter if he could allow me five weeks' time. But I was told that the letter was needed immediately. I do not think that the plan for my visiting Paris will materialize.*

Meanwhile, Professor Bose received a copy of his paper published in the Royal Society by mail and sent a copy of it to the editor of the famous journal *The Electrician*. However, Bose expressed his inability to write anything about his paper himself. Later, in the reply received by Jagadish Chandra Bose, it was surprising that the editor found this paper very important. He praised this paper and wrote a letter to the Royal Society for permission to publish this paper's abstract. This is what the editor of *The Electrician* wrote to Jagadish:

> *I am delighted with the most interesting and lucid abstract of your Royal Society paper. The subject is of such extreme interest, both scientifically and practically, at the present time, that I hope to be able to give prominence to the abstract at an early issue. I am writing to the secretaries of the Royal Society to obtain their sanction to the publication of your abstract.*

But Bose was distraught with the politics against him at that time and most of the people around him were engaged in humiliating him out of jealousy and malice. Bose was so upset that in a letter to his friend Tagore, he wrote:

> *Recently, I have been able to devise and construct a unique artificial eye. One can see various colours of light through it which one normally cannot. Besides, this eye can see red and blue lights distinctly. It is a bit amazing that it is slightly green-blind. I don't know how it has come to imitate your eyes.*

The artificial eye will be able to complement my theory of vision. The development of this eye will lead to many other interesting discoveries. But I doubt whether I will be able to complete those.

> *I feel fatigued, both physically and mentally and shall be happy accepting your hospitality.*

Burdened by these sorrows, Jagadish Chandra Bose went to Shilaidaha to his friend Tagore and spent two days there. Staying with a friend, his mind became very light. There was a lot of discussion on poems and science and moments of laughter were shared with Tagore's family. Returning to Calcutta with a lighter mind and better thoughts, he received the news that his name was one of the names chosen to go to the Paris Congress in the proposal made by the university. However, the Director of Public Instruction was not in favour of his going to Paris, even though Lieutenant Governor Woodburn was a well-wisher of Jagadish Chandra Bose. On 21 June 1900, Jagadish Chandra Bose wrote a letter to his friend Rabindranath Tagore that:

> *I wished I could get over my present mental condition. There has been no news from England yet (regarding approval to go to the International Physics Congress, Paris). If the delay continues, my going or not going will become meaningless . . . Would you please write a poem on this with the caption 'Trishanku's journey to Heaven'? It is extremely comfortable to stay in between the Heaven and Earth!!*

In the meantime, Professor Bose got approval from the Secretary of State for his foreign trip and he had only a few days left to prepare for going abroad.

Bose arrived in Paris and participated in the International Physics Congress. However, he was late in reaching Paris. Information about the subject on which he was to speak in the Royal Society reached there at the last minute and was not published till then. There was a doubt whether he would even be allowed to speak. However, the President of Congress came to Professor Bose and requested him to deliver the speech. In the speech, Professor Bose spoke very superficially about the topic without going too deeply, but many people liked his lecture very much. After this, the President of Congress requested Professor Bose to give a detailed speech on his subject, which was then translated into French. The President of Congress said that he did not know earlier that the subject was so important and beautiful. As the speech progressed, people in Paris became more interested in Professor Bose's subject, and Bose became more and more thrilled. In the end, the Congress President said that Bose's topic was brand new and it would take at least two years to propagate it. It will take time for people to accept it. He said one more thing, 'Physicists do not know physiology and physiologists do not understand physics. If you add psychology to it, then no one will understand anything. As the speaker said in the beginning, only the side of physics should be published.' Bose quotes it in his letter to Tagore written on 31 August 1900.

Since Physics was Bose's main subject, there would not be many questions about the specialization of the subject. He also said that the paper on Bose's speech would be published in the first edition of the *Proceedings of Congress*. The President of the Congress praised Bose's research, but he was also sceptical about how other subjects, especially physiologists, would accept this research. Jagadish Chandra Bose gave a speech here on 'Reaction of inorganic and living matter'. In this, he showed the fatigue experiments in receivers of electric waves. Leaving these receivers unattended for a while would bring their power back. In this paper, Professor Bose demonstrated the similarities and differences between inorganic substances and living beings for the first time. He compared the potential curves obtained at different temperatures in iron oxide with graphs obtained from living muscle, which had some fundamental similarities. He also observed that some inorganic substances behaved negatively with normal stimuli and some positively. They found these effects to be comparatively similar to those of the living.

A few days after the speech, Bose went to see the Eiffel Tower in Paris. Bose did not need a ticket to see the Eiffel Tower as he was a speaker of Congress and a guest of France, but he was looking to buy a ticket for his wife as her arrival was personal. Since Professor Bose knew only English and did not know French, he found it difficult to buy tickets. Jagadish and his wife were helped by a Frenchman who knew English and French. The man gave his visiting card to Professor Bose, and Bose also gave his card of gratitude to him. The gentleman hastily read, 'Bose!!!' and as soon as he read it, he shrugged and said – 'Bose! Definitely not Jagadish Bose!!' Professor Bose replied with a smile that the suspicion of that gentleman was correct and that he was Jagadish Bose. He was thrilled to hear this and excitedly told a lot about Bose to the person sitting at the ticket counter. He was angry with him for taking money from the special guest of his country while sitting at the ticket counter. Along with this, he also urged the person sitting at the ticket counter to return Professor Bose's money. A large crowd gathered there in no time, who were thrilled to see Professor Bose's venerable personality and special scientific research.

In the meantime, on 31 August 1900 from London, Bose wrote in a letter to Tagore:

> *I was delighted to see the influence of science in Paris but at the same time I got totally dejected when I remembered the prevailing state of affairs in my own country. The one who lags behind in the continuous, cruel and intense fight for existence, will gradually be weeded out and extirpated. What an earnestness I find here! As soon as the people come out to know of a new invention, they immediately go to use it. Those who first learn to use, they dominate and defeat the rest of the world in industry and manufacturing. This is an eternal fight going on throughout the globe for years.*
>
> *How long can an idle, unenterprising nation like us survive!*

Swami Vivekananda also came to Paris when Professor Bose was there, and there was a brief meeting between Swami Vivekananda and Bose. Swami Vivekananda went to hear Bose at the Congress. Listening to Professor Bose, Swami Vivekananda praised him and his wife and wrote in one of his letters (later published as a collection entitled *The Wanderer*):

> *Here in Paris have assembled the greats of every land, each to proclaim the glory of his country. Savants will be acclaimed here—and its reverberation will glorify the countries. Among these peerless men gathered from all parts of the world, where is thy representative, O thou, the country of my birth? Out of this vast assembly a young man stood for thee, one of your heroic sons, whose words have electrified the audience and will thrill all his countrymen. Blessed be this heroic son—and blessed be his devoted and peerless helpmate who stands by him always.*

At the Paris Congress, Dr Waller also presented his research paper on a similar topic to Bose's, titled 'Electric Current in the Eye of a Frog'. Both Bose and Waller were engaged in pushing the boundaries of knowledge further. Doctor Waller was trying to theorize that plants also have sensations and these feelings come into existence shortly after the seed has been planted. This is where there is a fine line between life and death. However, other physiologists were by no means ready to accept these things. Waller was branded as an eccentric. Waller also became irritable due to this. Once, a debate broke out between the followers of Bose and Waller. Waller's followers used to say that the line between life and death is in the seed four days after sowing. The followers of Bose said that the line between life and death lies in the seed's skin and it extends to the soil. You can imagine what would have happened afterwards! Bose's friends advised him to stay as far away as possible from Waller for at least a few months. But when does that ever happen among those working on the same subject? Bose and Waller met and Bose kept his stance very soft, leaving Waller stunned.

After finishing his trip to Paris, Bose came to England. Physiologists in London shrugged off Bose's work as ridiculous and irrational—they argued that there was no resemblance between the living and the non-living. During the debate, other scientists would tell Bose that whatever he said should be called magic, not science. There can be no greater disgrace for a scientist than to call his work magic. After long discussions and arguments, some scientists relented and told Professor Bose that his theory is the complete opposite of existing theories, so some physicists, chemists and most physiologists will strongly oppose the theory. Bose writes about these debates in a letter to his friend Tagore:

> *. . . Soon you will enjoy the fun of 'Abhimanyu's killing' by Saptarathi (seven charioteers)! Bravo Jantipi, Bravo Socrates' This poor soul representing your country is asphyxiating.*
>
> *But the representative you have sent will never show his back in the battle. He sees with his inner eyes that he is showered with blessings from all his countrymen . . . .*

During his visit to England, a speech of Professor Bose was kept in the British Association, Bradford. Its topic was on the parallels of the effect of electrical stimuli on inorganic and living things. Professor Oliver Lodge also came to listen to it. However, there is an earlier story to this as well. In February 1900, Bose published a paper in the *Proceedings of the Royal Society* entitled 'Electrical touch and molecular strain produced in the matter by electric waves'. In this, Bose tried to prove Professor Oliver Lodge's theory of conductivity and coherence as insufficient. Bose believed that only a theory based on molecular changes could explain the conductivity changes. After the publication of this paper, Bose's research and theory were praised and naturally, Lodge's theory was widely criticized. Bose felt that Oliver Lodge would ask him tough questions after his speech and dominate him.

One would have been horrified to see the seriousness on Professor Lodge's face. Professor Bose needed 3 hours to explain his theory adequately, but Bose had only one hour to prepare after a lot of hard work. Surprisingly, he was given only fifteen minutes to speak, during which Professor Bose tried to explain maximum things about his theory. Professor Oliver Lodge was sitting in the first row. As the speech ended, the building erupted with applause and the President of Congress praised Bose, saying, 'Bose is a noted scientist from Calcutta.' He then invited experts to put forward arguments in opposition to the principles in Bose's speech. There was silence as soon as the speech was over. Oliver Lodge posed tough questions to Bose and Bose answered those questions. Everyone was listening to this conversation in silence. Two stalwarts of the same subject were in front of them. Shortly after, Oliver Lodge said to Professor Bose, 'Your research is excellent and meticulous, keep it up.' With this, he asked Bose, 'Do you have plenty of grain? These are all very expensive equipment and of course, your team will be huge! Most importantly, you have a long life to make countless important inventions.' Bose just smiled upon hearing the questions and comments from Oliver Lodge and thanked Professor Lodge for his compliments.

The very next day, Professor Barrett came to meet Bose and said to him, 'We met some people (including Oliver Lodge) last night and we believe that your time in India is being wasted. Can't you come to England? Many chair professorships are vacant due to a lack of suitable candidates. There is currently a vacant professorship position at a very excellent university. Would you accept it? No one else can get it except you.' Jagadish was not mentally prepared for this question. He remained calm and asked for some time. Bose once again asked in a letter to his friend Tagore (10 Sept 1900):

> *Now, tell me what to do? On the one hand, the work with which I am involved now is at its outskirts, the results of which, I feel, will be unique but this cannot be continued in an amateurish way. For that, a lot of labour and favourable conditions are*

> *required. On the other hand, nothing can sever my longingness for my poor motherland.*

I cannot decide what's to be done. All of my inspirations lie in the affection of my countrymen—if that affection is shattered, what remains of me?

16

Beyond a Nobel: Unification of Living and Non-living

Gradually fellow scientists started accepting Jagadish Chandra Bose's research, but with a suppressed heart. Prof. Bose used to say that there were still many experiments to be done. This was just a simple beginning. When people heard about these new ideas, they kept thinking about them. In such a situation, Bose would have been more careful while giving a speech because saying something wrong would break people's trust very easily. Scientists were divided into many factions. Everyone had different views. At this time, J.J. Thomson was saying that the atom could be split because the cathode rays he was producing seemed to be composed of some broken particles from the atom. Many scientists were not able to digest the matter of the splitting of the atom. J.J. Thomson was facing the same opposition to splitting of the atom, just as Bose was facing while redefining the living and non-living.

The physiologists, in particular, were strongly against Jagadish's views. In every meeting, heated debates would be held. Jagadish had to utter every word with care. Oliver Lodge wrote to Bose:

> *Many congratulations to you for your very important and suggestive experiments—but go slowly, establish point by point and restrain inspiration.*

Lord Rayleigh wrote to Bose: *Not so quickly, go a bit slowly.*

When Bose spoke of some unpublished scientific results to Rayleigh, he said, '*How can you sleep over all this? Are you so certain of life? Write night and day and publish them at once!*'

Who can be so sure of life and what is its path? In the beginning, even Jagadish Chandra Bose was unsure if it was true. And whatever experiment he was doing, to what extent would it remain true? But gradually, after further discussions about experiments, Bose saw a ray of hope and started moving forward. After that, rays of hope came in front of Bose from every direction. He could not decide which subject to choose and which subject to leave for other scientists to work on. Bose wrote in a letter to Tagore:

> *Before leaving my country, I had no idea about the vast and limitless subject I had laid my hands on. I could not understand initially what strange truth lies in the half-said words of the theory I was going to propound. Now, when I started interpreting the meanings of the words, I find a ray of light has emerged from the darkness.*
>
> *Wherever I look, I find rays of hope in abundance. I won't be able to finish it in my succeeding births . . .!*

Life is unbelievable. As Bose was talking about his next life, his health started to deteriorate. Dr Crombie told Professor Bose that he needed to have a major surgery and that there was little to be done. He had to be on bed rest for at least five weeks. Bose's foreign tour was also slowly moving towards its end. Bose wanted to spend every moment there doing experiments and discovering some new knowledge. Once again, Bose was in a quandary. He wanted to write about four subjects. Bose tried continuously, but it was becoming difficult due to his ill health.

Meanwhile, the famous magazine *Science* wrote a lot to praise about Bose and his work.

In the meantime, he received two letters from Tagore, in response to which Professor Bose wrote on 2 November 1900:

> *India lies at the core of my heart. If I can do something staying here, I would consider my life to be worthy. I can understand the hurdles that would come in my way when I return to my country. If the mission of my life remains unfulfilled, I will bear that too.*

Meanwhile, Professor Bose received an invitation from the Royal Institution to deliver a Friday evening lecture where he gave a detailed speech about his new principles. Hearing these, some people even went so far as to say that if Bose's theories were to be accepted as true, then school and college books would have to be rewritten. Dr Waller, who researched on almost the same subject, initially disagreed with Professor Bose's theories. But after much deliberation, he admitted:

> *It seems that your work can spoil my work too. The truth is the truth and I don't care if I am proved wrong. I will dedicate my laboratory to you. Either teach me or let's work together.*

It was a delightful moment for Professor Bose.

Jagadish started designing one of his laboratories at the Royal Institution. He started to make his equipment. He knew that he would never find a laboratory of physiology in India. He thought of returning to India and then to keep coming back to England every three years. Thus, their equipment remained safe and their research work, which was not possible in India, continued smoothly.

Meanwhile, Professor Bose sent an application to extend his stay for some more time. In the interim, he also received an invitation from the Society of Arts to deliver a speech on 'Science in Ancient India'. Bose was very busy in England. His surgery was successful on 11 December 1900.

Professor Bose had requested a further extension of his foreign travel for a year, but he was only granted an extension of six months. Shortly before, Tagore sent Bose the first part of his book of short stories (*Galpaguchcha*). On 16 January 1901, Bose wrote to Tagore:

> *When shall I expect the second part of your book? Three stories from the first part have so far been translated. It is impossible to maintain the beauty of the language in English. What can I do? But still, the beauty of the story is there. Nowadays, the people here read with enthusiasm the short stories published from Sweden, Norway and Italy. I want to get your writeups published just to see how you stand compared to those.*

Bose narrated Tagore's stories to many of his friends, especially his story 'Chutti'. His friends would get emotional hearing Tagore's stories and they could find the people around them in the story's characters. Bose wrote to Tagore on 22 March 1901:

> *People will not believe if I tell them about my new discoveries and also, I do not think that I am capable of describing those in the current language. A new nomenclature has to be found out for my new discoveries. You have not yet coined the indigenous names.*

Another speech of J.C. Bose was planned in the British Royal Society on 03 May 1901. Bose was very worried about this speech. He wrote in a letter to Tagore:

Only seven days left before my acid test. It will be proved that day whether I can unfurl the flag of my country and live up to your expectations.

I do not know whether I will be able to explain the intricate subject clearly within an hour's time. I do not expect to be able to preach the greatest truth which lies under the vast subject of science within a few days.

The subject of my lecture at the British Association was on a new and very intricate concept on the electrical subject and naturally the physiologists could not comprehend at the outset. Moreover, they can hardly believe that the subject of physiology is a part of the subject of physics. The scientists and the Christians here know it for certain that life is something great, placed at a very high pedestal compared to the world of inorganic substance. I do not think that I will be able to weed out this age-old belief overnight.

But I am confident that I will be able to establish the truth through a method completely new which I have derived from a unique discovery of mine.

Once, I was dreaming of the day when people from abroad would visit the holy land of India in the quest of knowledge and wisdom. The hope remains unattained. I will have to come to my homeland empty-handed, leaving all my achievements back in this country.

Because our countrymen bask in the glory of past deeds. Whatever may be our downfall these days, we will remain content with our pasts.

Jagadish Chandra Bose's mind was fresh. He was a physicist first and was not burdened by the traditional principles of physiology. No biologist thought of poisoning any metal. Jagadish Chandra Bose conducted different experiments on non-reactive metals like zinc, copper and even platinum. It was astonishing that when Bose poisoned these metals, he got to see graphs like plants and living beings. For tin, oxalic acid was shown to be effective. Bose observed that high doses of poison reduced the response of metals. When he showed a graph in his speech, Professor Michael Foster, Cambridge's senior physiologist at the front, suddenly stopped Bose and said, 'What's new in this? This graph is like the response received from living beings. We have known about such knowledge for a long time.' Sir Michael Foster was stunned when Jagadish Chandra Bose replied, 'Sir, this is a response from a metallic tin.' He advised Bose to send these results for publication immediately. He opined that Bose should now acquire ownership of these results by sending them to the publication before showing them elsewhere.

After some time, an invitation came for Professor Bose's speech in the Royal Society. Shortly before the address, Professor Bose received a telegram from the billionaire owner of a well-known telegraph company. It was written that he wanted to meet Professor Bose at the earliest. Bose replied that he did not have time. Immediately, another telegram came from there saying, 'I am coming.' In no time, he appeared before Professor Bose. He had the patent form in his hands and he placed that form in front of Bose and said, 'You are requested to please not tell everything in your speech. There's a lot of money involved in all of this. Let's get the patents done for you. You have no idea how big of a mountain of wealth you are turning down! I will put all my money into it. I want only half of it.'

Writing about this in his letter to Tagore, Bose says:

> *This billionaire came to me like a beggar just to earn some more money. Friend, I wish you could see the craziness of these people with money—money, money and money all the time, how hungry! See, the work I have come here for is far more worthy than money—I have only a few days left, whatever I want to say, I don't even have the time for it. I turned down his offer.*

Representatives of all the major telegraph companies were present to hear Professor Bose's speech. Bose says that the billionaire would have the Bose's equipment with him if those people were under his control. When Bose was performing, the notes written by Bose also disappeared from there, which the representatives of these companies might have taken away.

After this, another speech by Professor Bose was held in the Royal Society. Sir Michael Foster himself read Bose's paper and Bose demonstrated his experiments. Dr Augustus Waller, a well known physiologist, became very angry with that speech. Because of this, Bose had to answer the opposition alone.

An incident that happened in the nineteenth century was very famous in the Royal Society. The theory of heat and mechanical energy being equal, put forth by the renowned scientist Joule, was rejected by the Royal Society, calling it unscientific at that time. Twenty years later, the Royal Society admitted its mistake and published the same paper in its *Transactions*. A scientist told Bose that if he had the patience to carry this new invention with him for a long time, people would listen to him one day. If he left it at the very beginning, this whole area will be lost. Bose feared that he would not be able to continue this experiment upon his return to India.

After recovering from the illness, Jagadish Chandra Bose threw himself into experiments. He worked at the Humphry Davy-Faraday Lab in England. Bose experimented with a variety of intoxicants, drugs and poisons in plants. He found that when plants are given chloroform, they stop responding just like living beings and after a certain time when they get fresh air, they start responding again. The surprising thing was that the graph obtained in the experiment with plants and animals was the same. By giving more chloroform, drug or poison, the response in plants stopped completely, which was very similar to that of animals.

He worked on Sundays for five months and took no leave, which had a terrible effect on his health. Bose complained of high blood pressure and doctors had to give strict instructions to Bose to stop his work and rest.

In the meantime, when Bose sent the translated short stories of Tagore for publication in a magazine, he received a reply that only the original works with the author's signature would be accepted. Bose wrote a letter to Tagore asking for his signature on the original works and jokingly mentioned that if Tagore's permission was allowed, he should send the compositions for publication with his signature!

Once again, Bose sent an application to the Government of India to extend his leave for two more years. The Under-Secretary said that there should be no problem with this. But when Bose got his reply, he found that the Under-Secretary had remarked that Professor Bose's work was excellent, but his leave could not be extended anymore. However, Professor Bose received a letter from the Anglo-Indian Council which read:

> *I will do as much as is conceivable for your leave, because to separate you from your work is a sin against science.*

After a lot of efforts, Bose got a short leave, but the funds were significantly reduced to so little that it became tough for Bose to stay in England. When Bose wrote this in a letter to Tagore, he sent help to Bose through the Maharaja of Tripura, due to which Bose was able to bear his expenses abroad.

In the meantime, invitations continued to pour in from various parts of England for Professor Bose to deliver speeches. In his condition and with the time given to improve it, Bose completed almost six years of work in just six months. After researching five subjects, he wrote a research paper:

1) On the continuity of the effect of light and electric radiation on matter (It was already proved that light and invisible radiation exert the same influence.)
2) On the similarity of mechanical and radiation pulls
3) On the new principle of the photographic process
4) On the electric response of inorganic substances
5) On three types of electrical conductivity

These papers were sent to the Royal Society for publication. Bose was thrilled to do research in physics and he was confident that no one would oppose the papers published on these subjects.

But in the matter of the relation between the living and the non-living, there was a lot of opposition towards Bose. Mr Swinton even went so far as to say, 'Your theories do not appear to be science but rather it appears to be esotericism.' A physiologist would say, 'We don't research dead things. We are physiologists.' Physicists and chemists considered themselves to be the messiahs of experiments. An eminent vegetable physiologist said, 'Electrical reaction is not possible in vegetables.' After this, Bose recorded the electrical reactions in vegetables and showed them. Because of Bose's research, the established laws of physiology were being proved wrong, so there was a lot of anger among the people and they were protesting against it. Against this opposition, Bose was the only one to prove his principles.

In the meantime, another important event occurred. Burdon Sanderson and Dr Augustus Waller were considered distinguished scientists of physiology in Europe. Bose explained some of his experiments in detail in his speech to the Royal Society. He pointed out that secondary plants also give electrical reactions. Hearing this, Burden Sanderson protested, saying that only the mimosa plant provides a reaction that is an electric response. He accused Bose of unauthorized use of physiology in his physics research. Bose's only answer to that was, 'Can a particular class have authority over the terminology too?' As a result, the publication of Bose's research paper was halted. The physiologists united against Bose. This young physicist had infiltrated the empire of established physiologists, which was unbearable.

One day, Bose met Professor Vines, the President of the Linnean Society. He accompanied Professor Huxley's successor, Professor Hornes, to visit Bose's laboratory. He was so pleased to see the experiments shown by Bose, that Professor Hornes said that if Professor Huxley were alive today, he would know that his dream had been achieved. Professor Vines also invited Bose to deliver a speech at the Linnean Society.

In May 1902, Professor Bose learned that Dr Waller and Burdon Sanderson had hatched a conspiracy against Bose, due to which the Royal Society had refused to publish his paper on 'Reaction in Plants'. By stealing Bose's discovery, Waller had published a paper last November. Bose was very sad to know this. He did not know about it for a long time and in the meantime, Waller's supporters began to criticize Bose and say that Waller had already published the research that Bose was showing. The issues discussed in the council were kept secret and Bose had great confidence in everyone. Because of this, he felt deceived. Incidentally, Bose had the papers of the speech given in this regard at the Royal Institution and the documents received from the Secretary of the Linnean Society. After a much-heated debate based on these documents, the Royal Society accepted Professor Bose's previously rejected paper for publication.

The Royal Photographic Society also invited Professor Bose to deliver a speech. Bose took advantage of this invitation to take photographs in the dark with the help of invisible waves. This invention was highly praised and people said that it would be a revolution in itself.

Bose was preparing for his forthcoming book *Responses in Living and Non-living*. After the book was designed, when it came to the matter of to whom it should be dedicated, Bose wrote to his friend Tagore and asked. There were two options:

To the people of our country, with love and service
Or
For countrymen, who would lay claim to the intellectual heritage of their ancestors

After leaving England in September 1902, Bose reached India on 11 October. Upon his arrival, Bose was awarded the 'Companion and Order of Indian Empire' by the British government.

In 1902, Swami Vivekananda's demise happened. Sister Nivedita (Margaret Noble), a disciple of Swami Vivekananda and a friend of Jagadish Chandra, whom he also considered his sister, became more involved in the campaign and efforts of Abala Bose, wife of Jagadish Chandra Bose, to educate women and girls. Jagadish Chandra Bose and Sister Nivedita met for the first time in 1898 and became friends. Sister Nivedita had also come to see Professor Bose's laboratory at Presidency College. She had helped in editing the books of Professor Bose. It is said that Sister Nivedita and Swami Vivekananda inspired Professor Bose to patent his 'artificial eye'. With Sister Nivedita, Mrs Sara Bull also came to serve in India. Bose used to call Mrs Bull 'Mother'.

Meanwhile, Bose recieved the news of Tagore's second daughter being ill. When Tagore's second daughter (Renuka Devi) was sick and had trouble breathing, Bose sent Tagore a device that converts oxygen into ozone with the help of an electrical spark emanating from the device. They found it easier to breathe when ozone was taken by mouth. Bose wrote about it in a letter to Tagore on 17 March 1903. Bose wrote to Tagore on 19 March 1903 that the intensity of his suffering was high because the scope of his relations was very limited.

Tagore had some land in Puri (Orissa), which he intended to give to Bose. Bose asked Tagore if he thought Bose had any interest in the land. He told Tagore that once he had thought of making huts there and keep visiting them occasionally. But according to Bose, going there without Tagore would be akin to imprisonment. That is why Bose thought that the land should remain with Tagore.

Professor Bose's first book, *Responses in Living and Non-Living* (1902), was published by Longmans, Green and Company, London.

Professor Bose took over teaching, administration and other responsibilities at Presidency College back in the country. He again became as busy as before but continued to find time for his research. He had to fix his equipment again and had to face many difficulties to make some new devices in India. After Bose went abroad from Presidency College, the people who worked for him in iron and wood also started working elsewhere. Bose found his old colleague, the ironsmith, to work. Since he already had a lot of work having started working elsewhere, Bose was late to do even small tasks. Thus, Professor Bose had to face many difficulties in starting his experiments at the College and even simple experimental set-ups took him a long time.

To deal with the criticism and scepticism from experts abroad, Professor Bose decided to experiment by creating more complex and accurate results. He wanted to test the response of plants to mechanical and electrical stimuli. In *Mimosa pudica*, a leaf shrivelling is visible when touched, but this was not expected in normal plants. Physiologists considered the mimosa a special plant, while Professor Bose expected that even normal plants should respond to mechanical and electrical stimuli. Bose had to create an instrument that could be used to test the movement of very light reactions to stimuli in plants. An instrument capable of observing such a subtle movement was not available. Bose designed a device for this task in which he used an 'optical lever'.

With the help of this device, he tried to prove that the stimulation of plants elicits the same response as in animals and living tissues.

In December 1903, Professor Bose sent his five papers one by one to the *Philosophical Transactions* of the Royal Society for publication. The Royal Society initially praised Professor Bose's experiments, but then rejected these five papers due to intense opposition from high-ranking experts. This time, Bose was out of England and could not clear the doubts by having a face-to-face conversation with an expert. Given his old association and personality, the Royal Society proposed putting the papers in its archives. This evasive refutation was in a way more dangerous to Bose's work, as it strengthened the sceptical view towards it in the scientific community. Critics of Bose's theories and research, thus, unitedly and intensely began to criticize it.

Then it was the year 1904. Bose's mind did not seem to work at all. All nineteen of his papers were yet to be published. Bose was sceptical of his publications. At the same time, Dr Waller published a book in which he wrote, 'Earlier people believed that only sentient plants responded . . . But such views have since then expanded and we have to admit that any vegetable protoplasm gives an electric reaction.' In this, Dr Waller repeatedly used the words 'me and us', but he did not mention where he got the inspiration for such an idea. He did not mention the name of Professor Jagadish Chandra Bose anywhere in the entire book. When Jagadish Chandra Bose questioned Dr Waller about this, he avoided the subject by saying that Professor Bose is basically a physicist (i.e., he is not authorized to say anything credible on physiology). In a letter to Tagore, Bose then wrote:

> *Can you imagine how deplorable science has become?*

At the same time, the fees for Indian children at St Xavier's College in Calcutta were doubled. The British government wanted to throw Indian children out of St Xavier's College. St Xavier's was the best educational institution in Calcutta at that time. Parents were worried about how their children would get a good education if Xavier's expelled them. Sisters Nivedita and Christine (another disciple of Swami Vivekananda) wanted to open a school at Rabindranath Tagore's house in Calcutta, but needed more financial help. Sister Nivedita had written a book that was popular in England. She hoped that the book's royalties would cover some of the school expenses.

Even after behaving contrary to his contemporary scientists, Bose did not give up. If the Royal Society rejected the paper, Bose took a different route. He planned to publish detailed books about his experiments. In 1906, his book *Plant Response* was published by Longmans, Green and Company, London. In this book, the experiments done during the three years of hard work and their results were described in detail. The book contained 287 scientific drawings and sketches. This book opened a new field in science and played an important role in establishing it. In 1907, another book of his was published called *Comparative Electro-Physiology*. This book was also published by Longmans, Green, and Company, London.

When Bose used to plan his experiments, he was faced with such questions—How to record the microscopic response of plants? How to register if plants are happy or sad under certain conditions with the help of instruments? How to produce the maximum response in an excited state with a very fine stimulator? Bose was a physicist by origin, so he had a more natural understanding of building instruments, preparing them to produce results with precision, etc., than a physiologist. Therefore, he was able to create high-quality equipment, which gave reliable results and was accepted by scientists on a global scale.

Bose published six volumes of books on the subject of correlation between physics and physiology. These books were published by Longmans, Green and Company, London, which described in detail the experiments and results done by Bose in about six or seven years. The first book, *Responses in Living and Non-Living*, had 199 pages. *Plants Responses* had 781 pages and the book contained descriptions of 315 experiments and their results. *Comparative Electro-Physiology* had 760 pages and included descriptions of 321 experiments and their results. After this, Professor Bose was inclined towards making more high-quality instruments. The book *Researches on the Irritability of Plants* had 376 pages and described 180 experiments and results. Then, the work *Life Movements in Plants* done in 1917 and 1918 was published in Calcutta itself, which will be mentioned later. All these books had a total of about 2500 pages and contained details of more than a 1000 experiments that Professor Bose had conducted concerning the existence of life and brain in plants as a result of research done in about ten years.

In the search for life in plants, Bose was the first to start looking for reactions in vegetables, because vegetables were considered to be the simplest plants in terms of reactivity. Bose's contemporary scientists were working on plants that were most active in terms of reactivity—*mimosa, desmodium* and insect-eating plants. Bose gave the 'theory of electrical organs' to these plants. Bose conducted a comparative study in which grapes and tomatoes were placed on one side and frogs, tortoises and lizards on the other, and Bose found that stimulating them recorded the same response from their tissues. After this, the 'conducting balance' was invented to measure the speed and timing of excitable signal transmission in these plants and living tissues. With its help, he proved the similarity in the electric responses given by the mechanisms of vegetables and the systems of living tissues. These experiments were so detailed, precise and accurate that it was not easy for physiologists to rule them out.

For a time, plants were considered mystical. It was difficult for botanists to standardize plant behaviour. Therefore, they were reluctant to treat plants as machines or bodies and openly opposed its theories. Jagadish Chandra Bose standardized the processes inside plants. He also recorded subtle reactions to stimuli in ordinary vegetable plants—experiments beyond the books of vegetable physiology at the time. The 'optical pulse recorder' made by Bose was superb and simple. Bose conducted experiments in plants with this device by varying the age of the plants, the weather, the temperature of the atmosphere and other factors. Plants did not respond after a period of time when Bose had given the stimulating factor too much, which Bose called 'death-spasm'. He found that the 'death-spasm' occurs at different temperatures in different plants and that the line curve of the response is different in different plants. He also found that 'death-spasm' occurs only at relatively low temperatures when the plant's response is due to some artificial reason (by excessive artificial activity or poison).

Bose found that in addition to mechanical movement in plants during 'death-spasm', there was also electric movement i.e., 'electric-spasm'. He recorded an 'electric death spasm' of up to half a volt in a pea grain. Bose once said mildly that if 500 grains of these peas were combined into a series, an electric shock of several hundred volts could be produced. Those who peel peas and make vegetables do not know how dangerous they are.

Bose also found similar automatic heartbeats in the heart muscles of telegraph plants and animals, which he tried to understand in detail in this comparative study. He found that this pulsation is affected in the same way by temperature, medicine and poison in plants as in animals. During the experiments, he also found that some chemicals, such as those used to increase heartbeat, were also increasing the rate of heartbeat in plants in the same way.

An interesting result was that, just as the pulsating muscles in animals were less affected by external stimuli than the normal muscles, the same was found in various parts of the plant of *Desmodium*. Professor Bose found innumerable results based on his experiments that were almost impossible for normal plant physiologists to digest. Influenced by Bose's work, where many scientists from all over the world were protesting, some scientists wanted to test this new breath of fresh air for themselves. At that time, the 'optical lever' developed by Bose was being used in some experiments at the University of Cambridge—Scientist van der Valk (Germany) was also repeating Bose's experiments in his laboratory, and Professor Harper of Columbia University, USA, was also doing experiments taking great interest in Bose's research topic.

Bose himself not only believed in research of a complex order but also wanted to inculcate the spirit of the quest for knowledge in the children of the country. At the same time, he wanted to make them energetic to complete the long and tedious journey of discovering new knowledge. Bose suggested setting up a workshop for children in Rabindranath Tagore's school. He had requested Tagore to arrange only Rs 1000. A small American lathe machine (for Rs 200) and a small kerosene engine (for Rs 100) would also come in this money. Jagadish Chandra Bose said there could be no greater work than making children capable adults. In a letter to Tagore, he wrote that it is my dream to have a workshop in your school. He said that without good teaching, machines and equipment are junk. He wanted the school to have excellent teachers as well.

In 1907, the government again allowed Professor Bose to travel abroad on a scientific deputation. Bose went to the best universities in England and America and gave speeches in front of outstanding scientists. During this visit, Bose mainly lectured on 'Mechanical and electrical reactions in plants' at the British Association, Dublin.

Meanwhile, Tagore's health had started deteriorating. Bose was very concerned about Tagore's health and he continued writing letters to him. He had promised Tagore in the letters that he would visit his residence frequently after coming to India.

By this time, many students from Bengal had started coming to England. Now, ochre-coloured Bengali people were often seen on the streets of London. However, here, Indians had to struggle a lot to save their existence.

After living in England till 1909, Bose went to America. He delivered a series of speeches to scientists at the prestigious American Association for the Advancement of Science and the Botanical Society of America in America. He also lectured on plant physiology at the Western Society of Engineers in Chicago and at the University of Illinois.

In 1913, Rabindra Nath Tagore was awarded the Nobel Prize in Literature. With joy, Professor Bose wrote to his friend:

> *19 November 1913*
> *Friend,*
>
> *I had been writhing in pain that the world had not laurelled you earlier. Now, the pain is no more. How shall I express my gratitude to Almighty? Pray, you become even mightier and remain a winner always. May god bless you always.*
>
> *Yours.*
> *Jagadish*

* * *

As soon as Rabindranath Tagore got the Nobel Prize, people from far and wide started gathering in Shantiniketan. A special train was started to reach Shantiniketan and Jagadish Chandra Bose presided over the gathering of people from far and wide.

After coming back to India, Professor Bose started working towards the development of super-sensitive instruments. He created the 'Resonant Recorder', which consisted of a steel wire with the help of which the movement of the plant was recorded on paper. With the help of this, Professor Bose measured the movement during the fall of the leaves of the *Mimosa*. The resonant recorder recorded a dot every 0.005^{th} of a second. In this way, the accuracy of its measurement of time was equal to 2000th of a second. But Bose wanted an even better device. Bose improved its design by making it 100 times better with a single lever and 10,000 times better by adding a compound lever. These were called oscillatory recorders by Bose. The results and graphs taken with the help of these recorders were so convincing that the Royal Society finally accepted Bose's research paper for publication in *Philosophical Transactions* in 1913. After publishing *Researches on Irritability of Plants*, invitations to deliver speeches from many foreign universities started pouring in and the government sent him on a scientific deputation again in 1914.

Bose also took his plants with him to show his experiments to the scientists on this foreign trip. Among these plants were mimosas and telegraph plants. In Europe, most plants go into hibernation when they freeze. It was no less challenging to carry delicate instruments made on his own on these foreign trips, since some plants were also included in them. A strange thing happened when these tropical plants were taken to the places of extreme cold. The sensitivity of these plants to extreme cold also had a profound effect on them. Bose was a great experimentalist. He sealed these plants in glass boxes and made special arrangements for the temperature and air in them.. Only half the plants survived the sea voyages. He was placed in the Regent's Tropical Green House when he arrived in London. Simultaneously, Bose established a temporary laboratory of his own in Maida Vale. Here, he began to study the changes when tropical plants were moved to cooler places.

At first, Bose was invited to speak at Oxford University, followed by a demonstration of speeches and experiments at the University of Cambridge. In May 1914, a Friday Discourse Lecture was also held at the Royal Society. Here, his resonant recorder recorded the communication in plants in the form of excitatory shaking. The oscillatory recorder recorded the beats of the plants and showed how they resembled living animals. The death recorder then recorded the death of the plant.

Many outstanding scientists and personalities came to visit Professor Bose's Maida Vale laboratory. One of these visits came from Sir William Crooks, the President of the Royal Society. Professor Crooks was an animal physiologist of the highest order. He was so impressed by Professor Bose's experimental demonstrations that he exposed one secret to Bose that day. Sir William Crooks said, 'Do you know whose casting vote prevented the publication of your papers on plant responses by the Royal Society?' Bose was unaware of this information. Sir William Crooks pointed out that it was none other than he himself who had opposed Bose's plant research in the Royal Society. He admitted that he didn't even believe that something like this could be possible at the time. He later accepted his mistake and acquiesced that Bose was right.

Mr Bernard Shaw, a well-known personality and a vegetarian, was deeply hurt by Professor Bose's findings because he believed he had not killed animals. The editors of many major newspapers also came to meet Bose and publish stories about him. The trip to England was a success. An invitation for Bose to deliver a speech also came from the Royal Society of Medicine in Britain. Bose's speech here was particularly appreciated and was said to be the beginning of another new branch in biology. Listening to the lecture, Sir Lauder Brunton wrote to Professor Jagadish:

> *Ever since I began the study of Botany in 1863 and still more since I made some experiments on the action of poison on plants in 1865, the movements of plants had a great attraction for me. For Mr Darwin I made some experiments on digestion in insectivorous plants in 1875. All the experiments I have yet seen are crude in comparison to yours, in which you show what a marvellous resemblance there is between the reactions of plants and animals.*

Bose then went to Austria (Vienna) and Germany to deliver speeches, where many opposing physiologists admired him. In Germany, he gave a series of speeches beginning in August 1914. After this, Professor Bose left for America.

In America, Professor Bose gave speeches at many prestigious universities. He lectured at the American Association for the Advancement of Science in Philadelphia, New York, the Washington Academy of Science and the American Bureau of Agriculture in New York. Surprisingly, Howard University organized the speech on behalf of the Departments of Philosophy and Psychology. Professor Stanley Hall, head of Clark University, was also interested in Bose's work.

During these visits, Bose's attention also turned to other reactions of plants. He wondered whether plants have a melancholy effect due to darkness. And, do plants feel better when exposed to light after dark? He was going largely towards plant psychology which was impossible at the time. Jagadish had the habit of walking on unknown paths. To prove the above, there was a need to build complex instruments measuring very subtle signals. Bose also conducted experiments in this direction and got very positive results. He did three experiments. He measured plants' growth under their wounding and observed the differences in their pulse-like activity. In the third experiment, he attempted to explore the possibility of paralysis when deep wounds were inflicted.

To measure all this, the professor made an instrument called a 'Crescograph' which was able to measure the microscopic growth in plants. Professor Bose found no significant difference in plant growth in the first two cases. Then, Bose saw this wound many times. When he pricked the plant four times with a needle, the intensity of the plant's signals being recorded decreased and the plant went into depression. It took two hours for the plant to recover from this depression. Cutting the plant with a knife affected its growth, which lasted for a few weeks. Many different types of plants showed different effects, such as some plants' leaves withered upon being left with linseed for several days when they were cut. Bose measured this signal in both the stalk and the leaf by plucking the leaves and found surprising results. The plants would remain affected for several hours. The stalk and plant recovered, but the detached leaf gradually died off shortly after.

Bose had said in one of his speeches, 'These are our mute companions, silently growing beside our door and they have now told us the tale of their life-tremulousness and their death-spasm that is as inarticulate as they. May it not be said that their story has a pathos of beyond any that we have conceived?'

If we compare the growth of plants with the things around us, the difference is very subtle. Plants grow one-millionth of an inch every second. A very fine and complex microscope is required to see a millionth of an inch. Such complex microscopes could not be made at that time. At that time, an instrument was used in plant science laboratories called the 'auxanometer', although this instrument could show only 20 times the size. One had to wait for several hours to see the growth of plants with this device. Bose created an excellent instrument for this task, which he called the 'high magnification crescograph'. This instrument not only magnified the movement in many ways, but it also recorded the movement. This instrument could record the activity by magnifying it ten thousand times.

However, Bose was not satisfied with the capabilities of this device. He changed it and made it better. Bose observed that the growth of plants did not happen in a linear form but rather it happened in a rhythmic way—like ascending and stopping in the form of beats. This was also new to plant physiologists. The Crescograph is counted among the most important inventions of Jagadish Chandra Bose. He did many important experiments with its help. They measured the effects of chemicals, drugs and poisons on plant growth with very high accuracy. They also measured plant growth in the presence of various stimulating factors and made important findings. He found that in some plants that were stimulated with an electric current, the growth was greatly accelerated. But growth was greatly reduced if the same electric current was passed through other plants. Many poisons were given to the roots of plants—the plants either died or their growth was greatly reduced, although the surprising thing was that by giving these poisons in very small quantities, the plants started growing more. These were completely new results from the point of view of pharmacology and medicine. Bose observed the effects of different amounts of poison even under different environmental conditions.

Bose was still not happy with his crescograph. He revamped it, making it even better to be able to see one-millionth of an inch in a second. The magnification might have been surprising at this time. Bose was a person who was never satisfied. He modified his crescograph and added a magnetic device to it, which increased the magnification power of the modified crescograph by 100 million times. Not only that, but its magnification power could be adjusted from 1 to 1000 lakh times as needed. Bose called it a 'magnetic crescograph'. In this, he used a weightless lever. The needle of this device moved at a speed of about seven lakh kilometres per hour, which was almost 24 times the speed of the bullet fired from the gun. Bose continued to use his magnetic crescograph for experimental demonstrations at large gatherings. With the help of this, he could clearly display the change in the growth of plants by making a slight change in the temperature of the plant chamber. The growth that had been affected by all these changes was easily visible. The audience would have it all like magic. In 1919, Bose again set out on a foreign trip. This time, with the help of his magnetic crescograph, the plants showed their growth even though they were in a dormant state in the severe winter of Europe. Microscopes had to wait a long time to get the magnifying power of this Bose crescograph.

With the help of this crescograph, Bose studied the effects of light, heat, chemicals, drugs, poison, touch, etc., on the growth of plants. This area of plant science is called tropism and it also has many types. He also tried to learn the expressions of plants under different conditions. What should be the name of this branch of science? At that time, there were many discussions about whether it should be called psycho-physiology or physiological-psychology. When science was divided into its own hierarchies and specialization was considered superior, Bose pushed the boundaries of broad science by breaking the boundaries of its branches. Jagadish Chandra Bose had to face stiff opposition so that today interdisciplinary or multidisciplinary sciences are respected. Bose laid the foundations of plant neuroscience. Professor Bose proved that plants have a nervous system. Because of him, it was also discovered that the nervous system of plants is of the simplest kind. Therefore, studying the nervous systems of plants at an early stage can be beneficial for studying the human nervous system.

In the beginning, the most significant gap between animals and plants was that plants do not have the nervous system tissue that carried information from place to place like animals, a notion that Bose's research proved to be baseless. It was another matter that the sensitivity of plants was much lower than others. Bose's high-magnifying crescographs and magnetic crescographs could measure the granular growth of plants. Still, some mathematical calculations had to be done to determine whether a stimulant increases or decreases the growth rate of plants. Bose intended to make these calculations automatic. He made such changes to his device that its needle started moving upwards or downwards according to the rate of growth. After many changes, the instrument that Bose made was called the 'balanced crescograph'.

With the help of this instrument, Bose could record about 70 millionths of an inch per second. It was kind of wonderful. It was like a dream to measure the microscopic growth of plants so precisely. With the help of a 'balanced crescograph', not only could a positive or negative change in growth rate due to a stimulant be seen, but it could also be known that, given the amount of this stimulant, whether the growth rate remained positive or not. Bose also measured the effect of light on plants. He also measured the response of plants to a very short flash of light. Bose included these experiments in his book and sent a letter to be published in the famous journal *Nature*. Bose also used his invisible rays to conduct experiments with plants. He conducted experiments on plants with different intensities of these rays. Some plants leaned towards light in winter and turned away from sunlight in summer. Bose showed that this is due to the increase and decrease of signalling in the nervous system of plants, just as it changes with increasing temperature in animals. He showed that plants are also dipoles like magnets, with their stems always growing upwards and their roots always downwards, i.e., one opposite to the force of gravity and the other gravitating towards it. If the new plant kept in the test tube is reversed, then after some time, the plant understands the force of gravity, and even if its roots were upwards earlier, they turn and start going down again and the stem starts moving upwards.

It was found that there are many such organs in plants that are always in motion, but their displacement is so subtle that it is not possible to see them. This displacement is quite evident in the morning and in the evening. It also happens because there is a change in light and temperature in those times. Once, when Bose went to his native land, Faridpur, the people there told him that there was a tree that slept at night not far from Bose's house. When Bose went there, he saw a palm tree bent sixty degrees due to a strong wind storm, but the upper part of its trunk had turned slightly and was straight towards the sky. In the night, the straight side towards the sky would bow down and people would say that the tree was sleeping. It would do the same thing in the morning and stand upright towards the sky. This tree was five metres tall and its trunk was twenty centimetres wide. The people of Faridpur considered it a divine and living tree. When Bose wanted to do a scientific test by putting his instruments in this tree, the people started opposing it after seeing his foreign-looking equipment. They were afraid that this might upset the divine power of that tree. They were later persuaded upon being told that the exotic-looking instruments were made by Bose himself in India and that his assistant, the priest's son, would install them in the tree.

But another question had come before Bose. Do plants sleep too? If not, does their activity also decrease at night like animals? To solve this problem, Bose designed a device that gave plants an electrical shock at an hourly interval and measured the magnitude of the response of those plants. Thus, Bose found that some plants are active late in the morning and remain active till late at night. At night, they start to tremble but do not lose their sensitivity completely and by morning, they stop responding to tremors. Bose found that the mimosa plant responds to a stimulating shock in 0.076 seconds, compared to eight times the time it takes for a slender frog to respond. Such findings are not familiar to us and even today, plants are considered slower than animals.

Bose was not satisfied with this. He began to search for 'memory' in plants. It was, in a way, very awkward in a traditional sense. Plants having memory was not to be readily accepted. Bose took two forms for this. In the first, memory had to come again and again. In the second, a memory was to fade away when there was a reason for it in some way. With the help of his instruments, Bose proved its presence. Later, it was called psycho-physics. Bose injured some plants by inflicting sharp blows on them and found that the blows left a permanent mark on the surface of their organs, which could not be seen by ordinary means and which remained in the plants in a hidden state only. Injured plants do recover, but these micro-injuries never heal. He also did similar experiments on the surface of metal plates in which he got positive results. Three important disciplines, namely Physics, Physiology and Psychology, were converging here. Bose improved upon Dr Bergson's 'memory' theories. But Bose did not stop here. Mentioning all of his research work here is impossible. His contribution in this field is phenomenal.

17

Foundation of The Bose Institute

The promise of the Government to establish an advanced laboratory of physics, which was made during Bose's initial research in the late nineteenth century, did not materialize till 1913. The files were deliberately delayed by the bureaucratic machinery. In 1913, Bose was about to retire from the services and during this time, the bureaucratic machinery again woke up. In 1914, the scheme was materialized for which Professor Bose had longed for his whole service period. An advanced laboratory of physics was established in Presidency College, Calcutta. Bose was nevertheless relieved that his students will benefit from the new facilities. But who will compensate for the time which was lost in the life of Bose? Bose had clearly wanted that it should not happen to any other young bright scientist in India again.

In 1913, Professor Jagadish Chandra Bose retired after completing fifty-five years at the Presidency College. However, the Bengal government did not want to let him go because of his influence on the students and the excellence in his research, so the tenure of Professor Bose was extended for two more years. Now, he was to retire in 1915. He was given the title of 'Emeritus Professor' and he continued to receive a salary in lieu of a pension. In 1912, he had already been awarded the 'Companion of the Star of India' award by the Government of India, which was considered the highest award given by the British government in its colony. Later, he was also given the title of 'Knighthood'.

On the day of his retirement in 1915, Professor Bose started efforts to establish a new institute based on his values and vision.

In 1914–15, he went to Europe and America on his fourth scientific deputation. He again gave speeches on his new research topic in universities like Oxford and Cambridge. He gave his third Friday Discourse Lecture at the Royal Society on 'Plant Autographs and Their Revelations'. He gave a speech on 'Action of Drugs on Plants' before London's Royal Society of Medicine. He then moved to the US and lectured to eminent scientists in the leading universities of the US, the prestigious American Association for the Advancement of Science and the New York Academy of Science. After that, he went to Japan and gave speeches at Waseda University. Returning to India, he delivered his inaugural address at the establishment ceremony of Banaras Hindu University on Vasant Panchami in 1916 upon the invitation of Pandit Mahamana Madan Mohan Malviya.

Bose wanted to establish a research centre as prestigious as the Royal Institution of England in India. But for this, there was neither sufficient economic self-reliance and resources nor did Bose have the time. Bose had put a lot of pressure on the government and able people to open research institutes of excellent quality in India. In 1909, Sir J.N. Tata started the Indian Institute of Science in Bangalore. At the same time, Tagore also wanted to establish a university where the best scholars from all over the world would come together and work. In the process, he started Visva-Bharati University, at Shantiniketan, Bengal.

On 30 November 1917, on his fifty-ninth birthday, he laid the foundation for Basu Vigyan Mandir. Bose invested his lifetime savings (approx. Rs 4 lakhs) to establish this institute. There was help from the government for constructing the building for this institute and for the annual budget. Professor Bose wanted an independent institute which supported its scientists in every way, where scientists could enter with full devotion in search of the truth. He wanted to focus on more research which could change the perspective of the world towards India and which could establish India as the leader. He wanted to overcome the bureaucracy and resistance which he had faced his whole life in this new institute for its students and scientists. He established a separate place where the indigenous equipment was preserved and displayed. On one hand, there was research going on in physical sciences and on the other hand, researchers were also performing research on different diseases, which was very crucial in India at that time. Professor Bose had a great vision towards communicating the ongoing research to the common public. There is a very large theatre with a well-equipped platform used to demonstrate experiments and oral lectures, which can accommodate 1500 people simultaneously. The design is such that there is no hindrance to the sound and visibility of the speaker. Sir Jagadish Chandra Bose himself was one of the greatest science communicators ever. His writings and lectures are proof of this statement. Basu Vigyan Mandir soon became famous for publishing scientific literature. The famous magazine *Athenaeum* wrote:

> *The foundation of an institute for research in pure science is an event in the history of India. The publication of the Transactions, the first fruits of its activity, shows that it is an event also in the history of science.*

It had been a very long journey since 1901 when scientists perceived Professor Bose's claims about the plant's response and his communication to the Royal Society as dubious, to the time of 1920 when Prof. Bose gained enormous prestige among scientists globally. A research institute of international standards cannot survive without endowment funds, so Prof. Bose tried hard to receive funds from governments and other sources. Sometimes, he succeeded and many times he failed, but he never stopped. He planned to seek support from the international intellectual community to support such an institute. Now, Bose Institute is a well-known research institute globally in several research fields.

Professor Bose continued his research in the year 1918. In the same year, based on his experiments, he published *Transactions of the Bose Research Institute, Calcutta*. The first edition came in the form of a book named *Life Movements in Plants*. Bose had now increased his travels in his own country. In 1918, he gave speeches at the Bombay Opera House on 'Unity of Life' and 'Invisible Light' at the University of Bombay. In 1919, the second edition of his book, titled *Life Movements in Plants*, came out of Basu Vigyan Mandir, in which the experiments done by Professor Bose were given in detail.

Bose and Tagore's friendship was now old and mature. When the brutal Jallianwala Bagh massacre took place in Punjab in 1919, several hundred Indian farmers, children and women who were peacefully protesting were surrounded and gunned down on the orders of General Dyer. Saddened by this dastardly incident, Rabindranath Tagore returned the title of his Knighthood received by the British government. On receiving this news, Jagadish Chandra Bose wrote a one-sentence short letter to Tagore:

* * *

2 June 1919,

Dear friend,
You are great.

Yours,
Jagadish

* * *

In 1920, he went to Europe for the fifth time and again lectured on his new research topics at Oxford and Cambridge. He was also awarded an honorary degree of LLD by Aberdeen University. He was also elected a Fellow of the Royal Society, London, on 13 May 1920. He was the second Indian to be elected a Fellow of the Royal Society. Professor Bose displayed his 'Magnetic Crescograph' here at the University College, London. He also went to France and Sweden, where he gave his speeches at various prestigious institutions. In the same year, Bose Research Institute published the subsequent two volumes of its *Transactions*. In the same year, *Avyakt*, a compilation of Professor Bose's speeches, articles and stories was also published in Bengali.

In 1923, he again went to Europe. This time, he went to England (Imperial College, University College, London), France, Czechoslovakia (Prague University), Denmark (Danish Botanical Society, Copenhagen University), etc., giving speeches and demonstrating experiments. In 1924, his *Physiology of the Ascent of Sap* and his fifth book, *Physiology of Photosynthesis* were published.

After returning to India, he continued to give speeches in convocation ceremonies at many universities, among which Banaras Hindu University was prominent in 1925.

In 1926, his sixth book, *Nervous Mechanisms of Plants*, was published which Professor Bose dedicated to his close friend,

Rabindranath Tagore. In the same year, he went to Europe on his seventh scientific mission. This year, the Belgian government honoured Professor Bose with the country's prestigious 'Commandeur Ordre de Léopold' honour. He participated in the Committee on Intellectual Cooperation of the League of Nations in Geneva (Switzerland) and lectured at the University of Geneva. Famous scientists like Albert Einstein and Professor Lorenz were also present at this speech given by Bose.

In 1927, his seventh book, *Collected Physical Papers*, came out. This year, he again went on his eighth trip to Europe. Two more books, *Plant Autograph and Their Revelations* and *Motor Mechanisms of Plants*, were also published. All these books were published by Longmans, Green & Company, London.

In 1928, he went on his ninth trip to Europe. After attending meetings and delivering speeches at many important places, he went to Egypt, where he lectured at the Royal Geographical Society of Egypt. In that year, 1928, he also delivered a speech at the degree distribution ceremony at Allahabad University and was also awarded an honorary degree of DSc. At that time, Professor Meghnad Saha, a disciple of Professor Jagadish Chandra Bose, was a Professor and the Head of the Department of Physics at Allahabad University.

In the same year, Rabindraath Tagore's health deteriorated, affecting him mentally. Despite being older than Tagore in age, on 22 October 1928, Bose wrote a letter to Tagore, which can be called a classic milestone of their friendship:

> *I am always concerned for the mental agony you are undergoing now. For the past thirty years, we two were close mates and colleagues. I feel hurt for your afflictions. I will consider myself fortunate if I can come to your any help in any capacity.*
>
> *Both of us have befriended our worst enemies. But it is difficult to have the strength of mind in a smaller arena where*

> *there are neither friends nor enemies. Even then, great deeds have been accomplished and will be accomplished in the future. Keep that in mind always. I feel our long-lasting friendship is a gift of God.*
>
> *. . . We will continue with our respective missions till we breathe our last. We will never be bogged down.*

In 1929, he went to Europe for the last time on his scientific mission. His tenth book, *Growth and Tropic Movements of Plants*, was published by Longmans, Green and Company, London.

Surprisingly, in the mid-1930s, the Foreign Minister of Patiala wrote a letter to Professor Bose informing him that the British government had halved the budget of the Bose Institute for the session of 1931–32 due to economic difficulties. He said that the financial burden on the government is increasing due to the development of new educational and research institutions in India, so the British government has decided to reduce the expenditure on academic matters in the country. Bose was very saddened to learn this. Who could have understood more than Bose that spending in the educational sector was one of the most important tasks in the country? Bose himself was keen to do something else on this matter, but he did not see the possibility of doing so. Ironically, in the same year, Professor C.V. Raman was awarded the Nobel Prize for the discovery of the Raman Effect.

In 1931, Professor Bose delivered a civic speech in the Calcutta Corporation in the presence of the then Mayor, Subhash Chandra Bose. He remained active in the literary domain of Kolkata.

In 1933, Bose edited the seventh edition of the *Transactions of the Bose Research Institute* and presented a series of speeches at the University of Baroda. In the same year, Banaras Hindu University honoured him with an honorary DSc. In 1934, Bose edited the seventh and eighth editions of *Transactions of the Bose Research Institute*. In 1935, Bose edited the ninth edition of the *Transactions of the Bose Research Institute* and this year the University of Dhaka awarded him an honorary DSc. In 1936, Bose again edited the tenth and eleventh editions of the *Transactions of the Bose Research Institute.*

In 1936, being a great admirer of Tagore and his efforts to revolutionize education in Bengal, Bose sent some financial help to Tagore's Visva-Bharati University.

18

The Scientific Sufi

Professor Bose was a great explorer. He kept going on vacations and tours since the time he was married, at least twice in a year, with his life partner, Abala Bose. Abala Bose was a true partner in moments of his sorrows, rejoices and struggles. She always accompanied him on his international tours. They travelled across the seven oceans visiting innumerable places with historic, scientific or sociological importance. They travelled mountains, plains and oceans together. One of the journeys is worth mentioning here. They were returning to India from their tour of Europe and America in 1915. The travellers quickly planned the visit to several Buddha Temples in Ceylon which is in Sri Lanka during their return journey. After reaching Colombo (capital of Sri Lanka), they visited Ceylon and went towards the north of Rameshwaram by Madurai and Thanjore to Trichinapally to Srirangam. During the visit at one place, Bose was invited to visit the innermost precinct of the temple, which was considered as the holiest among the holies. Professor Bose answered that he was not an staunch Hindu and no longer believed in caste and had lost in any case by his journeys to foreign countries across the sea, so he had no right to enter (the holiest part of) the sanctuary. But the priest replied, 'No, no, come in. You are a Sadhu.'

Jagadish Chandra Bose always kept himself involved in active research. He worked with the several research students and scientists. But his tireless working style affected his health negatively. He used to fall ill and his friend Dr Nilratan Sircar used to treat him and supervise him. Mrs Bose used to take care of him with the strictest discipline. Professor Bose had a house in Darjeeling and one in Giridih (then Bihar and now Jharkhand) including one in Calcutta. In winters, he would shift to Giridih as the winters were hard in Darjeeling.

In the year 1937, he planned to spend the winters in his house at Giridih and was busy editing the *Transactions of the Bose Institute* there. One day, he went for a bath in the morning and didn't come out from the bathroom for a long time. When Mrs Abala Bose checked in out of worry, his pulse was no more. After some time, the doctor also confirmed his demise. It was around 8.30 am of 23 November 1937.

His body was brought to Calcutta and cremated there. Bengal was saddened and a large number of ordinary and great people participated in the last rites of their beloved and respected luminary.

Mrs Abala Bose continued working for the legacy of sir J. C. Bose and the activities initiated by him till her demise in 1951. She contributed to the vision of Professor Jagadish Chandra Bose before and after him.

Professor Jagadish Chandra Bose was active in the search for new knowledge till his last breath. He not only contemplated on but made efforts for the interest and bright future of the country throughout his life. He was never satisfied as a person and remained like this till the last beats of his heart. He could never be bogged down by his opponents or adversaries.

A few lines were found written in Bose's diary. Neither the date nor the poet's name was written with the lines. It may have been written by Professor Bose himself:

The land beyond the sea!
When will life's tasks be o'ver?
When shall we reach that soft blue shore
O'ver the dark strait whose billows foam and roar?
When will we come to thee
The calm land beyond the sea?

One can imagine, his ideal Karna must have been waiting to welcome Jagadish on that shore and Karna must have hugged Jagadish with the greatest pride.

* * *

Bibliography

Chapter 1: Buried Sparks

1. **মন তুই রইলি খাঁচার আসে**: *Tofayell, Z.A. Lalon Shah and Lyrics of the Padma. Dacca: Ziaunnahar, 1968.*
2. **Buried sparks inside:** Dehlivi, Zahir. *Dastan-e-Ghadar: The Tale of the Mutiny*. Penguin Random House India, 2017.
3. **A vast *Buddha-Vihara* had been found in the excavations:** Mukherjee, Rila. 'History of Bangladesh: Early Bengal in Regional Perspectives (up to c. 1200 CE). Vol. 1, Archaeology, Political History, Polity. Vol. 2, Society, Economy, Culture, edited by Abdul Momin Chowdhury and Ranabir Chakravarti.' in *Asian Review of World Histories* 9, no. 2 (2021): 297–299.
4. **The famous Sufi saint Lalon Faqir**: *Jamal, Ahmed A. (eds.). Banglapedia: National Encyclopedia of Bangladesh (Second ed.).* Asiatic Society of Bangladesh, 2012.
5. **The British were able to suppress the revolt**: Dalrymple, William. *The Last Mughal: The Fall of Delhi, 1857*. A&C Black, 2009.

6. **It was the 30 November 1858**: Geddes, Patrick. *The Life and Work of Sir Jagadis C. Bose*. Longmans, Green, 1920.

Chapter 2: Facing the Fear

1. **In Faridpur, Jagdish observed**: Ray, M., and G. C. Bhattacharya. 'Acharya Jagadish Chandra Basu'. In *Kolkata: Basu Vignan Mandir*, 1963.
2. **The house was on fire**: Geddes, Patrick. *The Life and Work of Sir Jagadis C. Bose*. Longmans, Green, 1920.
3. **In the evening, a '*Jatra*' was organized:** Ibid.

Chapter 3: The Unconventional Mentorship

1. **Bhagban Chandra Bose set up a Bengali school:** Sen Gupta, D. P. 'Jagadish Chandra Bose: the man and his time.' In *Remembering Sir J C Bose*, pp. 1–62. 2009.
2. **The wound was so deep:** Geddes, Patrick. *The Life and Work of Sir Jagadis C. Bose*. Longmans, Green, 1920.

Chapter 4: Tryst with Karna

1. **Jagadish Chandra Bose used to tell:** Geddes, Patrick. *The Life and Work of Sir Jagadis C. Bose*. Longmans, Green, 1920.
2. **Till the end of his life, he remembered:** Ray, M., and G. C. Bhattacharya. 'Acharya Jagadish Chandra Basu'. In *Kolkata: Basu Vignan Mandir,* 1963.
3. **In the words of Jagadish himself:** Geddes, Patrick. *The Life and Work of Sir Jagadis C. Bose*. Longmans, Green, 1920.
4. **Jagadish used to remember the same of his father**: Ibid.
5. **Mughal emperor Jahangir changed its name to Badh-e-Diwan:** Burdwan Municipality Website (http://burdwanmunicipality.gov.in/).

6. **Pratap Chand Roy who published an English translation:** Roy, Pratap Chandra. *The Mahabharata of Krishna-Dwaipayana Vyasa*. Bharata Press (1889), 2016.
7. **Malaria took the form of an epidemic in Bengal around 1870:** Roy, Rohan Deb. '"An Awful, Unseen Visitant": The Return of Burdwan Fever.' *Economic and Political Weekly* 43, no. 12/13 (2008): 62–70.
8. **From that copper, Jagadish made a regular size**: Geddes, Patrick. *The Life and Work of Sir Jagadis C. Bose*. Longmans, Green & Co., 1920.

Chapter 5: Physics and the Father

1. **great personalities like Alexander Duff, David Hare:** Bellenoit, Hayden JA. *Missionary Education and Empire in Late Colonial India, 1860–1920*. Routledge, 2015.
2. **The first educational institution was opened:** Rao, Parimala V. *Beyond Macaulay: Education in India, 1780–1860*. Taylor & Francis, 2019.
3. **Calcutta Mohammedan College**: Trevelyan, Charles Edward. *On the Education of the People of India*. Longman, Orme, Brown, Green & Longmans, 1838.
4. **Sanskrit College in Varanasi:** Dalmia, Vasudha. 'Sanskrit scholars and pandits of the old school: The Benares Sanskrit College and the constitution of authority in the late nineteenth century.' *Journal of Indian Philosophy* 24, no. 4 (1996): 321–337.
5. **Raja Ram Mohan Roy wrote a scathing letter:** Roy, Raja Rammohan. "Letter to Amherst, 11th December 1823', in H. Sharp (ed.), Selections from Educational Records Part I, 1781–1839 (Calcutta: Superintendent Government Printing, 1920), 98–101.' in *Indian Responses*, pp. 1–4. Routledge, 2019.

6. **In 1817, Raja Ram Mohan Roy, Dwarkanath Tagore:** Kadir, Md. 'Progress of higher education in colonial Bengal and after—a case study of Rajshahi College (1873–1973).' (2004).
7. **A letter to Dalhousie:** Ghosh, Suresh Chandra. 'Dalhousie, Charles Wood and the Education Despatch of 1854'. *History of Education 4, no. 2* (1975): 37–47.
8. **Father Lafont has made a significant contribution:** Krishna, Venni V. 'The Emergence of the Indian Scientific Community.' *Sociological Bulletin* 40, no. 1–2 (1991): 89–107.
9. **A state-of-the-art laboratory was established in 1866**: Biswas, Arun Kumar. *Science in India*. Calcutta: Frima K.L. Mukhopadhyay,1969.
10. **With the assistance of Alexander Pedler:** Lourdusamy, John. *Science and National Consciousness in Bengal: 1870-1930 Vol. 8*. Orient Blackswan, 2004.
11. **Jagadish's interest in physics:** Saha, Meghnad. 'Sir Jagadis Chunder Bose, 1858–1937.' *Royal Society Publishing* (1940): 3–12.
12. **During his BA studies, Jagadish remained an average student:** Sen Gupta, D. P. 'Jagadish Chandra Bose: the man and his time.' *In Remembering Sir J C Bose*, pp. 1–62. 2009.
13. **A profound effect on the physical health of Bhagban Chandra Bose:** Mukherji, Visvapriya. *Jagadis Chandra Bose*. Publications Division Ministry of Information & Broadcasting, 1983.
14. **Unfortunately, the Bose family had to face another accident:** Geddes, Patrick. *The Life and Work of Sir Jagadis C. Bose*. Longmans, Green, 1920.
15. **Bhagban Chandra Bose started a Khadi weaving company:** Ibid.

Chapter 6: Science or Civil Services

1. **Be your own master**: Sen Gupta, D. P. 'Jagadish Chandra Bose: the man and his time.' In *Remembering Sir J C Bose*, pp. 1–62. 2009.
2. **He took charge of 'Pabna':** Bhattacharyya, Prantosh, and Meher Engineer. *Acharya J.C. Bose-A Scientist and a Dreamer Vol. 1*. Kolkata: Bose Institute, 1996.
3. **Rajput soldier became Jagadish's guru**: Ray, M., and G. C. Bhattacharya. 'Acharya Jagadish Chandra Basu'. In *Kolkata: Basu Vignan Mandir,* 1963.

Chapter 7: Unsuccessful Encounter with Medicine

1. **India's first medical college was opened in Calcutta:** Chatterjee, Shamita, Ramdip Ray, and Dilip Kumar Chakraborty. 'Medical College Bengal—A Pioneer Over the Eras.' (2013): 385–390.
2. **Prof. Ringer, the well-known hospital doctor:** Geddes, Patrick. *The Life and Work of Sir Jagadis C. Bose*. Longmans, Green, 1920.
3. **Jagadish wrote a letter to his brother-in-law Ananda Mohan Bose**: Sen Gupta, D. P. 'Jagadish Chandra Bose: the man and his time.' In *Remembering Sir J C Bose*, pp. 1–62. 2009.
4. **He was the 'first Indian Wrangler' of Cambridge University:** Sarkar, Hem Chandra. *A Life of Ananda Mohan Bose*. AC Sarkar, 1910.
5. **He also wrote a letter of recommendation to Christ's College:** Geddes, Patrick. *The Life and Work of Sir Jagadis C. Bose*. Longmans, Green, 1920.

Chapter 8: New Beginnings in Physics

1. **Theodore Beck, who later came to India and became the principal of Aligarh College:** Akhtar, Shamim. 'ALIGARH.' In *Proceedings of the Indian History Congress Vol. 79*, pp. 620–624. Indian History Congress, 2018.
2. **His boat got stuck in a strong gust of wind in the Shanklin Bay:** Geddes, Patrick. *The Life and Work of Sir Jagadis C. Bose*. Longmans, Green, 1920.
3. **Sir Lord Rayleigh was the professor who taught physics to Jagadish**: Bhattacharyya, Prantosh, and Meher Engineer. *Acharya J.C. Bose-A Scientist and a Dreamer Vol. 1*. Kolkata: Bose Institute, 1996.

Chapter 9: The Indian Dream

1. **Today, I came to know that**: Bhattacharyya, Prantosh (ed). *Acharya J.C. Bose-A Scientist and a Dreamer Vol. 4*,p. 349. Kolkata: Bose Institute, 1996.
2. **Professor Henry Fawcett, urging him to find:** Geddes, Patrick. *The Life and Work of Sir Jagadis C. Bose*. Longmans, Green, 1920.
3. **Lord Ripon was a supporter:** Palit, Ram Chandra. *Speeches and published resolutions of Lord Ripon, Viceroy of India, from June 1880 to May 1882*. (1882).
4. **Lord Ripon and the Ilbert Bill were vehemently opposed by British:** Dobbin, Christine. 'The Ilbert bill: A study of Anglo-Indian opinion in India, 1883.' (1965): 87–102.
5. **I am usually approached from below not above:** Geddes, Patrick. *The Life and Work of Sir Jagadis C. Bose*. Longmans, Green, 1920.
6. **He started the People's Bank of India:** Ibid.

7. **So much solar energy is wasted:** Bhattacharyya, Prantosh (ed). *Acharya J.C. Bose-A Scientist and a Dreamer Vol. 4*. p. 349. Kolkata: Bose Institute, 1996.

Chapter 10: Repaid Debts, Unimaginable Loss and A Writer

1. **Durga Mohan Das was also the leader of Brahmo Samaj:** Karlekar, Malavika. 'Kadambini and the Bhadralok: Early debates over women's education in Bengal.'*Economic and Political Weekly* (1986): WS25–WS31.
2. **When Englishwoman Annette Akroyd opened:** Borthwick, Meredith. *The Changing Role of Women in Bengal, 1849-1905. Vol. 2088*. Princeton University Press, 2015.
3. **The school later merged with the Bethune School:** Singh, Maina Chawla. 'Philanthropy, Voluntarism, and Women's Education in Colonial India: A Study of the Bethune School, Calcutta.' *Asian Journal of Women's Studies* 6, no. 3 (2000): 65–92.
4. **She could not get admission to Calcutta Medical College:** Sengupta, Subodhchandra (ed). *Sansad Bangali Charitabhidhan*. Sahitya Samsad, 1998.
5. **She started the job as a social worker:** Singh, Maina Chawla. 'Philanthropy, Voluntarism, and Women's Education in Colonial India: A Study of the Bethune School, Calcutta.' *Asian Journal of Women's Studies* 6, no. 3 (2000): 65–92.
6. **In search of the origin of Bhagirathi:** Bose, J.C. *Abyakto*. Bangeey Bigyan Parishad, 1921.
7. **The Runaway Cyclone:** Bose, J.C. *Abyakto*. Bangeey Bigyan Parishad, 1921.
8. **with title 'Palatak Toofan'.**: Banerjee, Suparno. *Indian Science Fiction: Patterns, History and Hybridity*. University of Wales Press, 2020.

9. **Mr Ray Bradbury wrote his fiction:** Lorenz, Edward. 'The Butterfly Effect.' *World Scientific Series on Nonlinear Science Series A 39* (2000): 91–94.

Chapter 11: Search for the New Knowledge

1. **Jagadish once read a book:** Lodge, Sir Oliver Joseph. *Signaling Across Space Without Wires.* 'The Electrician' Printing and Publishing Company, 1894.
2. **Maxwellian means one who believed:** Maxwell, J.C., 1861. 'On physical lines of force.' *The London, Edinburgh, and Dublin Philosophical Magazine and Journal of Science* 23(151) (1861): 12–24.
3. **When Heinrich Hertz published papers:** Baird, Davis, Richard I. Hughes, and Alfred Nordmann (eds). *Heinrich Hertz: classical physicist, modern philosopher. Vol. 198.* Springer Science & Business Media, 1998.
4. **Although Bose's student N. C. Nag explains:** Geddes, Patrick. *The Life and Work of Sir Jagadis C. Bose.* Longmans, Green, 1920.
5. **In May 1895, Bose sent the first paper:** Bose, J.C. 'On Polarization of Electric Rays by Double Refraction Crystals', *Journal of Asiatic Society of Bengal* 64 (1896): 291–296.
6. **The other research paper was on his equipment**, Bose, J. C. 'On a new Electropolariscope.' *The Electrician*, 36 (1895): 291–292.
7. **Jagadish Chandra Bose was invited:** Bhattacharyya, Prantosh (ed). *Acharya J.C. Bose-A Scientist and a dreamer vol. 4*. Pp. 349. Kolkata: Bose Institute, 1996.
8. **Jagadish was performing this demonstration:** Vendik, Orest G. 'Popov, Marconi and radio.' *Nature* 374, no. 6524 (1995): 672.

Chapter 12: Inventor of Wireless Communication: Papov, Bose or Marconi

1. **Mr Gutenberg is responsible:** Rees, Fran. *Johannes Gutenberg: Inventor of the printing press.* Capstone, 2006.
2. **The International Telegraphy Union was formed in 17 May 1865:** Balbi, Gabriele, Fari Simone, Giuseppe Richeri, and Spartaco Calvo. 'Swiss Specialties. Switzerland's Role in the Genesis of the Telegraph Union, 1855–1875.' *JEIH Journal of European Integration History* 19, no. 2 (2013): 207–226.
3. **Wireless telegraphy was probably first conceived:** Romeu, Jordi, and Antonio Elias. 'Early proposals of wireless telegraphy in Spain: Francisco Salva Campillo (1751-1828).' In *IEEE Antennas and Propagation Society International Symposium. 2001 Digest.* Held in conjunction with: USNC/URSI National Radio Science Meeting (Cat. No. 01CH37229), Vol. 1, pp. 10–13. IEEE, 2001.
4. **In 1789, an assistant to the physician Luigi Galvani of Bologna:** Pupilli, Gimlio Cesare, and E. Fadiga. 'The Origins of Electro-Physiology.' *Cahiers d'Histoire Mondiale. Journal of World History. Cuadernos de Historia Mundial* 7, no. 1 (1962): 547.
5. **the 'Electric Telegraph':** Ronalds, Beverley Frances. *Sir Francis Ronalds: father of the electric telegraph.* World Scientific, 2016.;
   Hubbard, Geoffrey. *Cooke and Wheatstone: and the invention of the electric telegraph.* Routledge, 2013.
6. **Samuel Morse demonstrated an improved version of the electric telegraph:** Bektas, Yakup. 'Displaying the American genius: the electromagnetic telegraph in the wider world.' *The British Journal for the History of Science* 34, no. 2 (2001): 199–232.

7. **Antonio Meucci demonstrated a telephone in Havana:** Campanella, Angelo J. 'Antonio meucci, the speaking telegraph, and the first telephone.' *Acoustics today* 3, no. 2 (2007): 37–45.
8. **The world's first telephone was patented:** Mercer, David W. 'The telephone: the life story of a technology.' (2006): 151.
9. **The exciting point is that after exactly two hours, Elisha Gray also reached the patent office:** Evenson, A. Edward. *The telephone patent conspiracy of 1876: The Elisha Gray-Alexander Bell controversy and its many players.* McFarland, 2015.
10. **Around 1851, another machine, 'Snail Telegraph',:** Baring-George, Sabine. 'Historic Oddities and Strange Events (The Snail Telegraph).' (1889).
11. **Mahlon Loomis, a dental specialist in America, filed a patent:** Salazar-Palma, Magdalena, Tapan K. Sarkar, and Dipak Sengupta. 'The father of radio: A brief chronology of the origin and developments of wireless communication and supporting electronics.' In *2010 Second Region 8 IEEE Conference on the History of Communications*, pp. 1–8. IEEE, 2010.
12. **David Edward Hughes in England:** Brown, G. Burniston. 'David Edward Hughes, FRS, 1831-1900.' *Notes and Records of the Royal Society of London* 34, no. 2 (1980): 227–239.
13. **Even before Maxwell's death, Oliver Lodge:** Mussell, James, and Graeme Gooday, eds. *A Pioneer of Connection: Recovering the Life and Work of Oliver Lodge.* University of Pittsburgh Press, 2020.
14. **I have discovered that:** David Runes, Dagobert, ed. *The Diary and Sundry Observations of Thomas Alva Edison.* Published by Greenwood Press, 1968.

15. **William H. Preece also falls into this category:** Bruton, Elizabeth. 'Something in the air: The Post Office and early wireless, 1882–1899.' In *Knowledge Management and Intellectual Property*. Edward Elgar Publishing, 2013.
16. **Hertz waves can be used in telecommunications:** *Crookes, William. Fortnightly Review*, pp. 174–176. 1 February *1892*.
17. **Oliver Lodge also made the most effective:** Rybak, James P. 'Oliver Lodge: Almost the Father of Radio.' In *Grand Junction*.
18. **Oliver Lodge was a direct rival of Marconi:** Raboy, Marc. *Marconi: The man who networked the world*. Oxford University Press, 2016.
19. **Augusto Righi, improved the transmitter:** Leone, Matteo, and Nadia Robotti. 'Guglielmo Marconi, Augusto Righi and the invention of wireless telegraphy.' *The European Physical Journal H* 46, no. 1 (2021): 1–28.
20. **Popov also accused Marconi of stealing the design:** Raboy, Marc. *Marconi: The man who networked the world*. Oxford University Press, 2016.
21. **Science is full of examples of the wrong attribution:** Ibid.
22. **Marconi came to London from Italy**: Ibid.
23. **This provisional draft was of twelve pages:** Ibid.
24. **On 2 June 1896, Marconi slightly improved the draught of the patent:** Ibid.

Chapter 13: Praise from the Greats

1. **Dear Professor Bose, I have sent your previous:** Bhattacharyya, Prantosh (ed). *Acharya J.C. Bose-A Scientist and a Dreamer, Vol. 4*. p. 285. Kolkata: Bose Institute, 1996.
2. **The then famous English newspaper *The Englishman*:** Geddes, Patrick. *The Life and Work of Sir Jagadis C. Bose*. Longmans, Green & Co., 1920.

3. **Meanwhile, Lord Kelvin, the famous physicist:** Bhattacharyya, Prantosh (ed). *Acharya J.C. Bose-A Scientist and a Dreamer, Vol. 4*. p. 286. Kolkata: Bose Institute, 1996.
4. **Indians do not have the natural nature necessary for science:** Geddes, Patrick. *The Life and Work of Sir Jagadis C. Bose*. Longmans, Green & Co., 1920.
5. ***The subject dealt with has long:*** Bose, Jagadis Chandra. *J.C. Bose and Microwaves: A Collection*. Bose Institute, 1995.
6. **From the above, I hope,:** Ibid.
7. **It has been settled that**: Ibid.
8. **Lord Kelvin, J.J. Thomson greatest mathematicians:** Geddes, Patrick. *The Life and Work of Sir Jagadis C. Bose*. Longmans, Green & Co., 1920.
9. **The Eastern mind was equally:** Sen Gupta, D. P. 'Jagadish Chandra Bose: the man and his time.' In *Remembering Sir J C Bose*, pp. 1-62. 2009.
10. **Interestingly, Marconi and Professor Preece met Professor Bose:** Raboy, Marc. *Marconi: The man who networked the world*. Oxford University Press, 2016.
11. **Professor Helmholtz, appreciated:** Sen Gupta, D. P. 'Jagadish Chandra Bose: the man and his time.' In *Remembering Sir J C Bose*, pp. 1-62. 2009.
12. **Professor Bose has left nothing:** Geddes, Patrick. *The Life and Work of Sir Jagadis C. Bose*. Longmans, Green & Co., 1920.
13. **The poem which Tagore:** 'Kalpana'. In *Rabindra Rachanabali* (Bengali), Vol. 7. p. 157. Calcutta: Visva-Bharati, 1975.
14. **Your first research results:** Geddes, Patrick. *The Life and Work of Sir Jagadis C. Bose*. Longmans, Green & Co., 1920.
15. **There is however, to our thinking:** Ibid.
16. **The originality of the achievement:** Ibid.
17. **To the great importance:** Ibid.
18. **It would be conducive:** Ibid.

19. **Being of the opinion that:** Ibid.
20. **He (Bose) is now drawing:** Sen Gupta, D. P. 'Jagadish Chandra Bose: the man and his time.' In *Remembering Sir J C Bose*, pp. 1-62. 2009.
21. **I learnt from Lord Rayleigh**: Bose, J. C. 'Patraboli (Letters of J.C. Bose)' (1994).

Chapter 14: Struggle Continues

1. **In 1865, just seven years after:** Maxwell, James Clerk. 'VIII. A dynamical theory of the electromagnetic field.' *Philosophical transactions of the Royal Society of London* 155 (1865): 459–512.
2. **He loved to write poems:** Bucci, Ovidio M., Giuseppe Pelosi, and Stefano Selleri. 'James Clerk Maxwell, the Poet [Historical Corner].' *IEEE Antennas and Propagation Magazine* 61, no. 2 (2019): 128–133.
3. **Lewis Campbell published a collection of poems by Maxwell:** L. Campbell and W. Garnett. *The Life of James Clerk Maxwell.* London: MacMillan, 1882.
4. **The smallest waves produced by Hertz:** Kraus, John D. 'Heinrich Hertz-theorist and experimenter.' *IEEE Transactions on Microwave Theory and Techniques* 36, no. 5 (1988): 824–829.
5. **Bose studied the polarization:** Bhattacharyya, Prantosh (ed). *Acharya J.C. Bose-A Scientist and a dreamer Vol. 4*. p. 285. Kolkata: Bose Institute, 1996.
6. **This research can be called:** Emerson, D. T. 'The work of Jagadis Chandra Bose: 100 years of mm-wave research.' In *1997 IEEE MTT-S International Microwave Symposium Digest*, Vol. 2, pp. 553–556. IEEE, 1997.
7. **In his following paper:** Bhattacharyya, Prantosh (ed). *Acharya J.C. Bose—A Scientist and a Dreamer Vol. 1*. p. 286. Kolkata: Bose Institute, 1996.

8. **Two scientists, Pearson and Brattain, wrote:** G. L. Pearson and W. Brattain. *Proc IRE*, 43 (1955): 1794–1806.
9. **He sent a paper 'On Self-Recovering Coherer:** Bose, Jagadis Chunder. 'On a self-recovering coherer and the study of the cohering action of different metals.' *Proceedings of the Royal Society of London* 65, no. 413–422 (1900): 166–172.
10. **Bose coined and defined terms such as 'electric touch':** Bose, Jagadis Chunder. 'On electric touch and the molecular changes produced in matter by electric waves.' *Proceedings of the Royal Society of London* 66, no. 424–433 (1900): 452–474.
11. **Dear friend, In the process of finding:** Bhattacharyya, Prantosh (ed). *Acharya J.C. Bose-A Scientist and a Dreamer Vol. 4*. Kolkata: Bose Institute,1996.

Chapter 15: The Great Friendship

1. **I had been to Belvedere on Tuesday:** Bhattacharyya, Prantosh (ed). *Acharya J.C. Bose-A Scientist and a Dreamer Vol. 4*. Kolkata: Bose Institute, 1996.
2. **Lieutenant Governor Sir J. Woodburn was visiting:** Geddes, Patrick. *The Life and Work of Sir Jagadis C. Bose*. Longmans, Green, 1920.
3. **You made a mistake in understanding me:** Bhattacharyya, Prantosh (ed). *Acharya J.C. Bose-A Scientist and a Dreamer Vol. 4*. Kolkata: Bose Institute, 1996.
4. **These are too surprising**: Bhattacharyya, Prantosh (ed). *Acharya J.C. Bose-A Scientist and a Dreamer Vol. 4*. Kolkata: Bose Institute, 1996.
5. **I feel ashamed to tell you:** Ibid.
6. **I wished I could get over with:** Ibid.
7. **Here in Paris, the greatest men:** Dwivedi, B. N. 'Swami Vivekananda's interaction with scientists and his appreciation

of them: Celebrating his 150th birth anniversary.' *Current Science* 106, no. 2 (2014): 315.

8. **Soon you will enjoy the fun of:** Bhattacharyya, Prantosh (ed). *Acharya J.C. Bose-A Scientist and a Dreamer Vol. 4.* Kolkata: Bose Institute, 1996.
9. **Do you have plenty of grain:** Ibid.
10. **Now tell me what to do?:** Ibid.

Chapter 16: Research Beyond a Nobel

1. **Many congratulations to you:** Bhattacharyya, Prantosh (ed). *Acharya J.C. Bose-A Scientist and a Dreamer Vol. 4.* Kolkata: Bose Institute, 1996.
2. **Not so quickly:** Ibid.
3. **How do you sleep:** Ibid.
4. **Before leaving my country**: Ibid.
5. **India lies at the core of my heart**: Ibid.
6. **It seems that your work can spoil**: Ibid.
7. **You are requested to please:** Geddes, Patrick. *The Life and Work of Sir Jagadis C. Bose.* Longmans, Green, 1920.
8. **To the people of our country:** Bhattacharyya, Prantosh (ed). *Acharya J.C. Bose-A Scientist and a Dreamer Vol. 4.* Kolkata: Bose Institute, 1996.
9. **Tagore had some land**: Bhattacharyya, Prantosh (ed). *Acharya J.C. Bose-A Scientist and a Dreamer Vol. 4.* Kolkata: Bose Institute, 1996.
10. **Professor Bose's first book:** Bose, Jagadis Chandra. *Response in the Living and Non-living.* Longmans, Green and Company, 1902.
11. **Bose designed a device for:** Gupta, D.P. Sen, Meher H. Engineer, and Virginia Anne Shepherd. *Remembering Sir J.C. Bose. Vol. 1.* World Scientific, 2009.

12. **The Royal Society initially praised:** Geddes, Patrick. *The Life and Work of Sir Jagadis C. Bose.* Longmans, Green, 1920.
13. **In this, Dr Waller repeatedly used the words:** Chatterjee, Susmita. 'Acharya Jagadish Chandra Bose: Looking beyond the Idiom.' *Science, Spirituality and the Modernization of India* (2008): 65–95.
14. **Can you imagine how deplorable:** Bhattacharyya, Prantosh (ed). *Acharya J.C. Bose-A Scientist and a Dreamer Vol. 4.* Kolkata: Bose Institute, 1996.
15. ***Plant Response* was published:** Bose, Jagadis Chandra. *Plant response as a means of physiological investigation.* Longmans, Green and Company, 1906.
16. **another one of his books was published called:** Bose, Jagadis Chandra. *Comparative electro-physiology: a physico-physiological study*. Longmans, Green and Company, 1907.
17. **After this, the work 'Life Movements in Plants' was done:** Bose, Jagadis Chandra. Life movements in plants *Vol. 1.* Bose research institute, 1919.
18. **There is also electric movement:** Bose, Jagadis Chunder. 'Plant and Animal Response: Occasional Lecture.' *Proceedings of the Royal Society of Medicine* 13, no. Gen Rep (1920): 101.
19. **A small American lathe:** Geddes, Patrick. *The Life and Work of Sir Jagadis C. Bose.* Longmans, Green, 1920.
20. **I had been writing in pain that the world:** Bhattacharyya, Prantosh (ed). *Acharya J.C. Bose-A Scientist and a Dreamer Vol. 4.* Kolkata: Bose Institute, 1996.
21. **After publishing his 'Research:** Bose, Jagadis Chandra. *Researches on irritability of plants.* Longmans, Green and Company, 1913.
22. **Sir William Crooks said, 'Do you know who:** Geddes, Patrick. *The Life and Work of Sir Jagadis C. Bose.* Longmans, Green & Co., 1920.
23. **Mr Bernard Shaw, a well-known personality:** Ibid.

24. **Ever since I began the study of Botany:** Ibid
25. **These our mute companions:** Ibid.
26. **Bose called it a 'magnetic crescograph:** Bose, Jagadis Chunder. 'Researches on growth of plants.' *Nature* 105, no. 2646 (1920): 615–617.

Chapter 17: Foundation of The Bose Institute

1. **Action of Drugs on Plants:** Geddes, Patrick. *The Life and Work of Sir Jagadis C. Bose*. Longmans, Green, 1920.
2. **delivered his inaugural address at the establishment of Banaras Hindu University:** Bhattacharyya, Prantosh (ed). *Acharya J.C. Bose—A Scientist and a dreamer Vol. 3*. Kolkata: Bose Institute, 1996.
3. **The foundation of an institute for research:** Geddes, Patrick. *The Life and Work of Sir Jagadis C. Bose*. Longmans, Green, 1920.
4. **Dear friend, You are great:** Bhattacharyya, Prantosh (ed). *Acharya J.C. Bose—A Scientist and a Dreamer Vol. 3*. Kolkata: Bose Institute, 1996.

Chapter 18: The Scientific Sufi

1. **No, no, come in. You are Sadhu:** Geddes, Patrick. *The Life and Work of Sir Jagadis C. Bose*. Longmans, Green & Co., 1920.
2. **The land beyond the sea:** Bhattacharyya, Prantosh (ed). *Acharya J.C. Bose—A Scientist and a Dreamer Vol. 4*. Kolkata: Bose Institute, 1996.

Acknowledgements

The writing process of the biography of Sir Jagadish Chandra Bose has been a life-changing experience for me. It started in 2015 when I was working at Indian Institute of Technology, Kharagpur. The urge to know more about Professor Jagadish Chandra Bose was ignited during a discussion with Prof. C.N.R. Rao at Jawaharlal Nehru Centre for Advanced Research, Bangalore. And the urge kept growing polynomially as I discovered more and more about Prof. Bose.

I am deeply grateful to the Bose Institute (Basu Vigyan Mandir) in Kolkata for maintaining rich archives of Professor Bose's works and related academic materials. I am grateful to Bose Institute for publishing the collections of academic and personal writings of Prof. Bose as *Acharya J.C. Bose: A Scientist and a Dreamer* in several volumes. I am thankful to Prof. Uday Bandyopadhyay, director, Bose Institute for permissions to use quotes and pictures from the archival texts of Bose Institute.

I am obliged to the work of Sir Patrick Geddes for writing the first biography of Sir J.C. Bose in 1920. Sir Geddes was also an academic scholar of repute and a friend of Sir J.C. Bose.

I wish to record my deepest gratitude towards all the people and organizations who came through and helped in the process of collecting resources and academic literature in writing this book.

I am grateful to Prof. Ranjana Aggarwal, Director CSIR-National Institute of Science Communication and Policy Resources, New Delhi, for her kind guidance and unconditional support.

I wish to record my thanks to my friend Dr Saawan Kumar Bag for helping me learn Bengali so that I could read the available relevant literature about Sir J.C. Bose in the Bengali language.

I am grateful to Vishnu Vijayan for going through the manuscript and his valuable suggestions to update it.

Presenting this book in the current form was not possible without the contributions of Chirag Thakkar and his team at Penguin India. I am deeply thankful to Chirag and his team for the editing and production of this book. I also owe a thank you to Penguin Random House India for publishing this book.